T0365596

Metamorphosis

A POETRY MANUAL FOR SURVIVORS OF CHILDHOOD SEXUAL ABUSE

ROBYN APFFEL

authorHOUSE®

AuthorHouse™
1663 Liberty Drive
Bloomington, IN 47403
www.authorhouse.com
Phone: 1-800-839-8640

Published by AuthorHouse   10/23/2014

ISBN: 978-1-4969-4602-7 (sc)
ISBN: 978-1-4969-4599-0 (e)

To my Sister Survivors:
for the struggles and the successes
that we all share,
for the strength that has sustained you thus far,
for the love, life, and laughter
you are sure to find in your future.
Your voices will be heard.

CONTENTS

Introduction..xiii

Part I **The Early Years, Accountability** 1
Don't Be Afraid 7
Daddy... 9
Song and Dance 10
Other Girls...11
Small Shoulders 12
Four Sisters 13
Train Track Lives...14
The Same Last Name......................................15
Against Her Will...16
Violation 17
Permission Denied...18
Magic Touch 20
On the Outside 21
Humpty Dumpty.. 22
Acts of Treason.. 23
Terms of Surrender 24
The Puppeteer.. 25
I'll Play Your Game 26
Somewhere Else... 27
What Will Happen? 28
Somehow I Just Knew 30
Whom Are You Protecting? 31
Where Is Your Baby Doll?............................. 33
Using Writing Prompts 34
Writing Prompts for Part I, The Early Years,
Accountability...35

Part II   **Twelve to Twenty, Developing
Survival Strategies**...................................... 37
What Do You Think?..................................... 45
My Body 46
Body, Mind, Spirit 47
It Ought to Hurt 49
Mirror, Mirror... 50
School Days 51
La Habana.. 53
Teacher's Pet 54
A Fine Family 55
The Observer 56
Cliques and Niches 58
A Few Good Friends..................................... 60
Seven o'clock in the Morning 61
At the Bus Stop 63
On Guard 65
Boxed 66
Emotional Armor... 67
Hold Me, Please 68
Fly Away..71
Innocence Retained 72
In His Hands..74
The Sweetheart Tree......................................75
I Don't Know Anything About That 76
Border Patrol... 77
Great New World 78
Daisy Won't Tell 80
Put Down the Pen and Turn Off the Music ...81
Guilty as Charged... 82
Twenty/Twenty... 84
At the Top of the Stairs 86
Writing Prompts for Part II: Twelve to
Twenty, Developing Survival Strategies 87

Part III Courtship and Marriage, Pre-Recovery ... 89

Personal Ad 97

Worthy of My Trust 98

If This Is Love 100

As Much as I Can 101

You Need to Know 102

One Wooden Horse Alone 104

Marriage Vows 108

A Map for the Journey 110

A Stranger in Paris 113

Sharon's Secret 115

Nothing of Significance 117

Chameleon 119

Barbie and Ken 121

Patchwork 122

Three Paces 124

China Doll 126

Rosanna 128

Tears Alone 130

Mechanical Advantage 131

A Different Touch 132

A Spectator Sport 134

A Taste of Honey 137

Complaint Department 138

Old Flannel Pajamas 139

Pas de Deux 141

Writing Prompts for Part III: Courtship and
Marriage, Pre-Recovery 144

Part IV Body Issues, My Physical Realities 147

More than That 153

Housekeeping 154

Take Good Care of Yourself 155

embodied 156

flight or fight 158

learning to breathe 159
They Say 160
Satisfaction 163
The Human Machine 164
Lies I Tell Myself 166
old habits 167
Going to the Hairdresser, and Other Acts of
Courage 170
Getting Naked 172
Perfumes and Powders 174
grooming 175
Reach Out and Push Away 177
Hugs and Kisses 178
An Exercise in Yoga 179
A Friendly Touch 182
Wonderland 183
Silhouette 184
masculinity 185
without inhibitions 187
it's my pleasure 188
Someone's Fantasy 189
Writing Prompts for Part IV: Body Issues, My
Physical Realities 191

Part V   Recovery, Substantial Healing 193
I Don't Know How 207
Contained in My Brain 208
Chaos 210
It 212
Feeling with a Limp 213
Only Words 215
Something to Say 217
I'm in Here 220
This Is My Reality, and Welcome to It 222
Journalism 224

paper truth 227
Shipwreck 229
Reconnecting the Circuits 232
Deciding to Grow 236
Don't Tell Me How to Heal!........................ 238
The Stone.. 240
Metamorphosis 242
Short Cut... 244
A Lot of Answers 245
I'm Not Finished 248
The Menu.. 249
A New Pair of Glasses 253
Call Me Robyn... 254
The Prodigal Son 255
The Lost Sheep 257
Never Far Away 259
Biorhythm...261
What I Need to Learn 263
Home to My Heart...................................... 265
Faces 267
Spiritual Connection.................................. 269
Dreamless Sleep 271
If I Share My Tears 273
Waiting for Me...274
I Love What I Am..276
As If It Should Matter.................................278
Jigsaw... 280
I'm Not that Easy to Love........................... 282
Growing Together 284
You Were with Me 286
After Eighteen Years of Marriage 288
Unveiled.. 290
Cloak of Innocence 292
Thou Shalt... 293
Closer to Love... 294

Time and Place 297
Reflections on Gifts 298
The Pearl 300
My Own Hero 301
The Grown-up Within 304
Fifty Things I Do Well 306
wisdom 308
The Living Water 309
I'd Rather Be Strong 311
Intentional Living 314
Negotiation 315
Tomorrow's Memories 316
Tomorrow Morning 317
Predictable Surprises 319
Living by Imagination 320
Stages of Life 322
Durable Dreams 323
Personal Mission Statement 324
Writing Prompts for Part V: Recovery,
Substantial Healing 326

Epilog 331
Acknowledgments 335

INTRODUCTION

Poetry speaks in the many voices I need to express the fears and heartbreaks of my child self, the struggles of my adolescent being far beyond the norm of self-searching and rebellion, the uncertainty of my trembling bride persona, and my evolving adulthood. Poetry synthesizes the fragments of my life that never dared to visit one another. Poetry crystalizes insights that I never knew I had and verbalizes feelings that I never allowed myself to experience. Poetry touches the core of truth in ways that a mere recitation of facts could never do, because poetry concerns itself more with verity of impact than with accuracy of detail.

The poems in this book do not constitute an autobiography, for, while they are essentially true and presented more or less chronologically, they are, first and foremost, poetry, which, by nature, contains an element of the imagination and a revelation of the universal. The medium of poetry allows me the paradox of both proximity and distance. I can stand intimately close to the emotion of my situation, while at the same time I can maintain enough distance from the intensity of my feelings to be able to withstand them. Poetry is intense; because of its brevity, it has to be. A twenty-line poem may equal approximately twenty pages of very powerful prose. The reader will quickly discover that these pages must be consumed in very small doses, one or two poems at a sitting. They need to be digested slowly, and that process is an exhausting one. They will be seasoned with many tears and they will be translated into the reader's own language by bringing her closer to herself than they do to me. Indeed, the author of these poems will disappear completely in those pieces that truly touch the reader's heart.

The language of my poems is highly accessible, as I write for communication with sister survivors, not for critics or poets. It is, nevertheless, fine poetry that employs a wide variety of technique and standard literary tools, but the images are clear and straightforward. The poems are still, however, highly interpretable, and herein lies the true gift from me to the reader. If these poems were nothing more than my story, I would write them only for myself and not for publication, but they represent much more than my own personal history; they chronicle the process of healing from sexual abuse, following the common steps that take us from injury to wholeness.

The process of writing this book, unlike the journey of life itself, was very orderly. I began writing this book at the age of forty-six, well into my own healing process, having counseled with my family doctor, several therapists, a few ministers, and many friends; having also read every book and article I could find on the subject; and having watched as many television talk shows, documentaries, and dramas on the topic as I could stand. I feel fortunate to live in an era in which sexual abuse is finally openly discussed and for which much information and support is available. Is this book different from all the others? Absolutely. First of all, it's mine. No one else has written or can write the poems that have emerged from my heart. Second, the format of this book is different from any other that I have seen. It is not merely a collection of poems on the topic of sexual abuse. It is a painstakingly constructed diagram of the therapeutic process I underwent in order to remediate the damage caused by my sexual abuse.

Childhood sexual abuse short-circuits the normal developmental stages. The purpose of therapy is to provide understanding and to fill in the gaps. I am not a psychologist, but I am a survivor and I understand the process. The poems in this book have been very deliberately arranged to reflect the order of human development and the steps of therapeutically working through the residual issues of sexual abuse. I am a teacher, so I began as I ask my students to do, with an outline, designating major and sub-topics to be addressed. A glance at the table of contents will quickly reveal the outline of this book. My original plan for this work remained remarkably intact from start to finish. When I started writing, I began with "The Early Years" by filling in poem titles beneath the appropriate sub-topics and then I constructed the poems themselves. A few poem titles were altered or deleted, and others added. What amazed even me was that when I had finished writing about the early years, I found that I was completely done with my necessary therapeutic work on the early childhood issues, and had nothing left there to be resolved.

And so I moved on to the "Twelve to Twenty" chapter, following the same procedure, with the same results; likewise, the pre-recovery issues of courtship and marriage. And then I hit a brick wall: "Motherhood." Nothing I wrote was any good. I was still in the middle of raising my three sons, and my efforts to be sensitive to their privacy left the poems sounding flat, insincere, and emotionless, not at all the way I felt. The issues I had with my parents may have left me feeling inadequate to the task of motherhood, but they never translated into issues with my own children. My three sons were innocent and delightful and wonderful, and I did not want to do them any disservice simply because I did not have good role models for parenting. I decided not to include a chapter on motherhood and moved on to the chapter about my body issues, also a difficult topic, but one that I forced myself to tackle precisely because I needed to accomplish some major healing in that area of my life. Since recovery is ongoing, I have never grasped the sense of having completed that section, and many recovery poems were written out of sequence as the spirit moved me and were then placed where they seemed most appropriate.

Although I entered into the course of writing with a clear view of what I wanted to write, my poems have served me very well by clarifying my own thinking. Much of what ends up in poetry is our subconscious knowledge, whether of a long-buried memory or a mature insightfulness. Imagery, the use of unusual phrases, and vivid metaphors often land on a page and look back at a startled writer. In literature classes we smugly give brilliant interpretations of classic works, claiming to know what an author meant or what events in his or her life may have inspired a certain line, but I must tell you that in re-reading my poems several times after several years, I have been surprised to find meaning in my own words of which I had not been consciously aware when I wrote them. Writing poetry can be a free word association exercise that releases tightly reined emotions, revealing to ourselves how incredibly well we have managed with this lousy lot life has dealt us, and we begin to stand a little bit taller, to make eye-contact with the people around us who used to intimidate us, and to speak more confidently. Through our own poetry, we discover who we are at the very core of our beings.

We also connect with others through the words of poems that evoke common emotions. The details of my life are unique, but when I write from inside the fear of a child, anyone who has ever been a child can respond to that emotion. The purpose of my publishing my poems on the process of healing from childhood sexual abuse is to lead the reader to respond, first by feeling the common emotion, and second by writing her own story. Writing prompts are given at the end of each chapter to suggest possible writing activities, but I encourage the reader to respond frequently to what she reads, and not to wait until the end of the chapter nor to limit her reaction only to the prompts that I direct. Any time there is a strong emotional response to a particular poem, word, or phrase is the time to sit down and write.

The greatest beauty of personal poetry lies in its total freedom of expression. There are no rules. Length is not at all a consideration. There is no need to follow grammatical conventions nor to be concerned with meter or rhyme. All vocabulary that is acceptable to the writer is suitable, and no subject is taboo. Overwhelmingly, secrecy about the abuse has caused the most significant and deepest wounds, and committing the truth of our lives to paper is the most courageous act of self-expression we will ever perform. The silence that was perhaps our ally in our youth is our greatest enemy in adulthood, and it is often excruciating to unearth the words to express what for us has been inexpressible. Poetry may be the language of love, but it may also be the language of outrage and indignation. There are words in every language for everything we have experienced, and in personal poetry we don't need anyone's permission to use them. The writer chooses her own words, and while some may be comfortable using crass or vulgar language, others may feel debased by using them, feeling that the words are in conflict with who they are. Readers need to respect the right of the author to self-expression without judgment. For some, hurling obscenities at the abuser just might serve the purpose of removing the dirt that was heaped upon them, unwelcome and uninvited, and throwing it back at the perpetrator. The important thing is to let your own writing reflect who you are, and not what someone else has told you that you must be. If my writing makes you angry, then harness that anger and write your own story.

For the most part, my poems are not very graphic, by design. There is little of shock value in my poetry because for impact I rely on the tension created by applying opposite forces within the same poem, but if you want to shock others with your writing, then you should go for it. A dear friend who has read all my poetry characterized it by saying, "At times you are lyrical and at others you have an ability to use words like weapons. Your poems are at once soft and hard, beautiful and angry." His evaluation pleased me greatly because it showed that he grasped my foundational reason for writing in the first place. Writing deeply personal material can be terrifying, but it is also liberating and healing.

I do strongly urge that anyone who is reading this book as a survivor of sexual abuse do so in conjunction with or following the process of professional therapy. In no way is this book to be considered a substitute for therapy. It may, however, help to speed up the process or deepen or clarify its meaning. A survivor may find in these poems just the right words to unlock doors that have kept shrouded the clues to health or growth, or perhaps will pose the right questions that need to be addressed. The order of the poems might suggest the level of healing already attained and a future path to follow. The poems may even help clarify what issues are real for an individual as well as what issues do not need to be worked on. In ancient Hebrew tradition, it was believed that to call something by its name gave one power over it. When we learn to call our abuse and our feelings by their proper names, even if veiled in the allusions of poetry, we do gain a sense of having control of our lives. That is precisely why we talk in therapy; words are powerful, and the words of poetry are exceptionally so.

The usefulness of this book is not confined to survivors of sexual abuse. Therapists can use the book as a springboard to open up conversation with patients who have difficulty finding the words to express their feelings. Spouses, partners, grown children, friends, or relatives of someone who has been abused can use it to help them better understand this person they care so much about. The issues that we survivors struggle with daily are rather mysterious to those around us who have never lived them. Even the most devoted of our confidants misses much of what we say due to distractibility and the overwhelming nature of the messages we transmit. The written word provides for them the opportunity to revisit.

Teachers and counselors who deal with children, knowing that several children in every classroom have been or are being sexually abused, can gain some insight by reading this book. Clergy, who must minister to both the abused and the abuser, may find some nuggets of truth to assist them. Abusers or potential abusers can discover how their actions affect their victims. Law enforcement personnel, attorneys, judges, and legislators can learn from the words of these poems the extent of the damage caused by the actions of the abuser, and perhaps reconsider archaic, patriarchal attitudes of the law toward perpetrators of sexual assault.

We live in a violent society that for too long has denied its lack of character by refusing to acknowledge the rampant existence of the unspeakable crime. When primarily women, but some men as well, finally dared to speak openly about childhood sexual abuse, survivors experienced a brief moment of sunlight, soon cast over by the shadow of allegations of false accusations and implanted false memories, resulting in the re-victimization of men and women who had been silenced by the shame that rightfully belonged to the perpetrators. I believe the statistics that one-third of American women and one-fifth of men will be sexually abused by their eighteenth birthdays. There are many degrees of sexual abuse, but not even the lowest degree is tolerable. I consider myself truly fortunate that my memories of my abuse have always been crystal clear and that when I confronted my father about the abuse, he did not deny it. I ache for those whose memories are hazy and for those whose abusers claim that it never happened. When I write poems about abuse, I do not attempt to delineate degree. Abuse damages, period. What I write in my poems is about the process of accountability, repair and forgiveness, and knowing and learning to trust oneself. My poems are about relationships at their best and at their worst; they are about love and caring, growth and triumph; they are about life, with all its imperfections, that is still worth the effort and still worth risking making human connections that just might turn out to be beautiful; they are about life as an unfolding, blossoming process that includes unthinkable insults countered by both well-ordered and serendipitous healing; they are about humanity at its weakest and at its strongest; they are about hope.

PART I

THE EARLY YEARS, ACCOUNTABILITY

Ah! The poetry of childhood! Idyllic, delightful, carefree! Yeah, right! Of course, I had some days like that. I remember singing happy tunes as I swung in the maple tree; I remember laughing with my family and friends; I remember trips to the shore, candied apples for Halloween, monster Christmases, and my first bicycle. I remember wanting a Ginny doll for my birthday and getting six of them with lots of clothes and a carrying case. I remember when my oldest sister wrote and illustrated a book for me when I was six years old and I remember having a tea party once with my mother, Blue Willow miniature dishes, with cola and chocolate cookies. I do have some pleasant memories for sure, and some day I might write about them because certainly they all were important to me and helped make me who I am. Indeed, it is those very moments that helped me survive the rest and taught me to treasure little bits of goodness wherever I could find them. My parents gave me life and they gave me my value system, even if some of it was by default. Although the poems in this chapter do not deal with my happy moments, it does not imply that I had none. The happy moments gave me something to hold onto; happy moments and words.

Words have always been my anchor. I remember things in words and dream in words. Words gave me the ability to hold onto my history until I was able to deal with it. My memories have not come to me in pictures, flashbacks that light up the silver screen for a moment and then disappear. The narrative of my childhood has always been accessible to me whenever I wanted to replay it.

Feelings were quite a different matter. As a child I learned to block my feelings whenever my father molested me just to ensure my emotional survival. I covered for him and kept the secret by wearing an unreadable mask. Just a couple of years ago I told one of my grade school teachers the truth about what had happened to me because I was curious whether anyone at school had been aware of what was going on in my household. He had had no clue. I guess I was a good little actress, but feelings are tricky and we can have them without even realizing it ourselves. At the age of forty-five I began reclaiming feelings about my abuse that I had never allowed myself to experience while it was occurring.

The poems in this chapter expose the fear and vulnerability of a child, powerless in her attempts to stop the abuse, yet with the conviction that she must protect the very person who is abusing her. The child does what she has to in order to preserve the family system that keeps her alive, and in the process she sacrifices her own childhood. None of her choices is a deliberate strategy; she merely copes the best way she knows how, instinctively choosing silence rather than confrontation. In her understandable immaturity, she does not truly comprehend her violation, though she has a feeling that something here is terribly wrong. She continues to trust her abuser because she has to trust him to protect her; what she doesn't know is that she needs him to protect her from men like himself, and he, of course, is not doing that. This child is not as wise as many of the poems suggest, for she does not possess the insights expressed by the adult writing them some forty years after the fact. Children live all of life in the discovery mode; all they know is what they have experienced, whether it is war, poverty, abuse, or peace, wealth, and care. Children can cope with and accept just about anything that won't kill them. But they certainly don't always thrive on it. The task of parents during the early years is to help their child walk into the world confidently and trusting in others; the parent who abuses his or her own child sends that child forth full of self-doubt and fearful of other people. When the initial developmental stage has thus been short-circuited, all subsequent stages are in jeopardy.

The wisdom of a child is her innocence. "Where ignorance is bliss," wrote Gray, "'tis folly to be wise." Children don't recognize abuse, but they are damaged by it nonetheless, the damage follows them into adulthood, and it is not easily repaired. The first step in reparation is seeing the damage, and our personal mirrors are very adept at denying its existence. We tell ourselves, "Sure, my father raped me, and he was a real bastard to do that to me, but it didn't hurt me . . . I'm okay." I may be okay at the very best, not likely, but I want to be more than just okay. Perhaps I did manage well as a child and perhaps I appear to be a happy, healthy, successful adult in spite of what was done to me. Is that enough? Not for me. I want to thrive and be completely whole. I want to walk through this world with confidence and I want to trust the people around me to talk to me truthfully and to watch out for what is best for me, as I want to do for them. I want to love deeply without fear of being hurt beyond what I can bear. I want to be forgiving so I can move ahead, unfettered by the disappointments and heartbreaks of the past.

My therapist asked me once after reading one of my poems, "How long did it take you to write this?" I answered, "My whole life." I could not have written any of these poems when I was twelve or twenty or even thirty-five. I needed to reach a certain point in my own healing process before I could even think of writing about my abuse issues. That point came in my mid-forties, when it was no longer possible for me to keep up the pretense of not having been damaged by the sexual abuse inflicted upon me by my father. By middle age I had grown tremendously and had experienced much success in life; I was in a reasonably good marriage with a good man whom I loved and who loved me back; I had three happy, well-adjusted sons; I enjoyed a good standing in the community; I had wonderful, loyal, supportive friends; I had a job that I liked and I did it well. But I was still terrified by life and I was still just pretending that everything was just peachy, that everything in my life was better than good, it was perfect. Since I was unable to accept anything less than perfect, I had to define perfection by what was and then declare it perfect. The lies that I had lived as a child had finally caught up with me, and I recognized them as lies, and I vowed that I would not live with them any longer. And so I set out to write the truth, about the sexual abuse and the damage it caused me, damage that I was determined to obliterate completely with no more denial.

The poems in this chapter are about early childhood, beginning with the abuse, which for me occurred around the age of eight. About one-third of the poems is written in first person with the child telling her own story. Few of the poems are narrative, as they express ideas rather than events. The voice of the child is sometimes accusative, sometimes questioning, sometimes pleading; it is innocent and vulnerable and confused.

Another third of the poems in this chapter is written in second person, either asking or telling the listener, who, in most cases is the child, what to do, how to feel, or what to think. The voice is sometimes that of the father or the mother, or sometimes that of an unknown, unidentifiable person. My purpose in writing some of these poems in second person is to show how little control an abused child has over her own actions, thoughts, and feelings. Healthy parenting encourages a child to act, think, and feel autonomously.

The final third of the poems is written in third person, usually referring to the child simply as "She." The use of third person allowed me as the writer to distance myself from the emotions and to see them with a more objective perspective than I would have had writing in first person. Often I write in third person when I have originally attempted a first person poem with no success. I consider poems that sound whiny as unsuccessful, so if a poem has that tone in first person I will rewrite it in third person, usually with great improvement.

In writing the poems for this first chapter I avoided narrative poems intentionally. I have read many books on the topic of childhood sexual abuse and have been disturbed by the details of what has been done to these little bodies. There is absolutely a place in this world for such descriptions, and I believe that the world ought to know the extent of the torture inflicted upon children so that reasonable adults will do everything in their power to put an end to this shameful behavior. I chose not to write the details of my own abuse; to do so would not have enhanced these poems. As the reader reacts to my poems, she may choose to write the details of her own experiences and not be influenced by mine or anyone else's. I talked with my counselors about the details of my abuse, but I did not record that information in my poems. Particularly for survivors of sexual abuse, it is unnecessary to read the details of someone else's horror in order to relive one's own, and so I chose to concentrate instead on the common feelings of desperation, fear, and powerlessness. However each one of us has experienced those feelings is its own story, connected by the emotions we have all felt.

DON'T BE AFRAID

The darkness in this room frightens me.
Everyone else in the house is sleeping but me . . .
And him. I hear his bare footsteps
Creaking up the stairway,
One step at a time, slowly,
Prolonging my agonizing fear.
My door that never had a lock swings open,
Its frame filled with his hulky gray shadow.

Don't be afraid, Dear,
It is only your father.

He stands by my bed now and stares down at my figure,
Naked beneath all these layers
Of blankets, sheet, robe, and nightgown,
Such useless protection.
He lies heavily on top of me
And silently strips me of my dignity
As easily as he strips me of my garments.
I close my eyes and hold my breath and turn off my brain
Until it is over, and then
His hulky gray shadow retreats through the doorframe.
It is even darker now
And the darkness in this room terrifies me.

Don't be afraid, Dear,
It is only your father.

I know.
That's what I'm afraid of.

DADDY

The word sticks in my throat now,
But that is what I used to call you . . .
Daddy.
Eight years old, and I was little and weak
And you were big and strong.

Daddy was my hero, my teacher, my friend;
Daddy was to be trusted;
Daddy was to protect me;
Daddy was to love me even if I did something wrong
Because I was your little girl.

But you didn't want a little girl;
You had no need for a child's adoration;
You had no patience with my struggles to grow;
You did not care for my dolls and tea parties;
You placed no value on my innocent love.

You should have known that I was too young
To have my trust in you destroyed.
I needed you to guide me, not abuse me;
I needed you to love me, not pretend that I was your
    lover;
I needed a father; I needed a Daddy.

SONG AND DANCE

Sing for me, Child:
Not your nursery rhymes
Nor the songs you learned at school;
But sing for me love songs
Filled with a passion
That you have no way to understand.

I know you're just a child,
But for now I need you to be a woman,
So sing for me a womanly song.

Dance for me, Child:
Not your tap lessons
Nor the folk dance you learned at school;
But dance with erotic movement
Filled with a passion
That you have no way to understand.

I know you're just a child,
But for now I need you to be a woman,
So dance for me a womanly dance.

OTHER GIRLS

Other girls play hop-scotch,
    Jump rope, leap frog,
        Hide-and-go-seek;
But I just try not to be found.

Other girls giggle
    And laugh till they'd die,
        Share silly secrets;
But I just try not to cry.

Other girls play house,
    Pretend to be grown-up,
        To be just like their Moms;
But I just try to grab a slice of childhood.

Other girls hug and kiss
    Their fathers
        When they say, "Good night,"
But I just try to avoid being touched by mine.

SMALL SHOULDERS

On the beach on a towel she sits,
Her arms crisscrossing her chest
As her hands inquiringly trace her own small shoulders,
Reddened by the noonday sun.
At his request, she smooths lotion
Onto her father's back and broad shoulders
As he lies facedown on a blanket in the sand.

She observes with great interest
As a man down the beach
Easily hoists his laughing daughter,
A girl about the same age and size as she,
Onto his glistening bronzed shoulders.
He carries her pail and shovel in one hand
As he uses the other to balance the girl
As he jogs along the water's edge.

And she wonders how it is
That her own small shoulders
Are expected to bear her father's weight.

Four Sisters

Father in his high-back Gothic chair
Sits like King Haakon, surveying the banquet table
    before him.
On the side chairs are Ingrid and Marta on the left,
On the right Kristin and Gretel,
All young and delicate,
Tender and sweet,
Strawberry blonde
With complexion of peaches and cream,
Lips of rosé wine.
The vision of the smorgasbord fuels Father's appetite
As he carefully considers
Which of these lovely delicacies
He will sample first.

TRAIN TRACK LIVES

Side-by-side with three years between us
We traveled through early sisterhood
Up sheer mountainsides, down into cavernous valleys,
Through dark, uncertain tunnels,
Chugging along parallel trails.

Our eyes never met and our paths never crossed
As you rolled along your rail
And I rolled along mine,
The same ties that held us together
Keeping us always distant, apart.

We had no choices, you and I;
We just did what the engineer directed.
He gauged our speed;
He determined our destination;
He decided when we should go or stop.

And you and I simply chugged along our parallel paths,
Barely aware of the other's presence,
Rarely speaking to one another,
Never reaching out to touch,
Unable to break free of our trip down the tracks.

THE SAME LAST NAME

They grew up in the same house
With the same parents,
But if they have the same memories
No one would ever know it.
They have never shared
    their experience, their pain,
        their fears, their joys,
            their dreams, their failures,
                their thoughts, their feelings.
All they have ever really shared
Is the same last name.

AGAINST HER WILL

Could she actually want him to do it?
She isn't kicking or scratching or screaming.
She doesn't cry;
She doesn't even object.
She does exactly what he asks of her
And allows him to do whatever he wishes
As she simply lies there
Stiffly limp.

His eyes are filled with lust,
Lust for control, and hers, if he cares to notice,
Are overflowing with fear and confusion.
She acquiesces under his power
Not because she wants to
But because she has to.
He is her father.

VIOLATION

For parking illegally, a five-dollar fine.
For speeding, make it fifty.
Caught embezzling? Restitution, cost of court,
    five years in prison.
Assault will get you five to ten;
Armed robbery, ten to fifteen, hard time.
Get fingered for raping a stranger
And you could spend twenty years in the pen;
But if you rape your daughter
She probably won't even report it . . .
They rarely do . . .
But don't count on it;
Times are changing.

PERMISSION DENIED

If you'd asked me, I would have told you
I don't want you to touch me that way.
It doesn't hurt; it simply feels wrong,
And in my innocence I don't know why.

I've barely begun to figure out
Where you end and where I begin.
I still see myself as part of you,
But something inside me feels terribly violated.

It wasn't so long ago that you'd undress me
To get me ready for my bath,
But now you just stare at me
And run your hands all over my naked body.

You touch me in places that everyone covers up
And you put my hands inside your clothing.
I feel something there that I don't recognize,
And I don't like how it feels but you won't let me let go.

You don't ask me if you can hug and kiss me;
You just press your mouth against mine
And push your tongue down my throat
Until it feels like I'm going to choke.

You hold me closer and tighter than I want to be held
And you move up and down, back and forth,
In a kind of rocking motion that feels nothing at all
Like when I used to sit on your lap on the rocking chair.

If you'd asked me if you could use me
To satisfy your urges and your need for power,
I don't know how I could have answered
Because you never gave me permission to deny you.

MAGIC TOUCH

Your magic touch charmed me.
You created the illusion of warmth and tenderness
And I convinced myself
That you were offering me much needed comfort.

Your magic touch cast a spell on me
And I obediently believed
That fantasy was reality,
That abuse was caring, and that sex was love.

Your magic touch bewitched me
Into seeing what I wanted to see.
You used trickery, and I saw wonder;
You used manipulation, and I saw strength.

Your magic touch deceived me,
Fooling my very senses
So that I would trust the sorcerer
And deny my own thoughts and feelings.

Your magic touch enchanted me
And with your highly skilled legerdemain
You took my childhood and transformed it
Into pain and confusion.

Your magic touch pulverized me.
You took your final bows and exited victorious
Leaving me alone, bewildered and humiliated,
To try to form a life out of my brokenness.

ON THE OUTSIDE

On the outside there's a smile,
But it's a lie,
For it only masks a deep sadness
That she stores up in her heart.

On the outside there's a willingness to please,
But it's a lie,
For it only covers a profound insecurity
Caused by her powerlessness.

On the outside there's tranquility,
But it's a lie,
For it only blankets an angry sea
That boils and churns inside her.

On the outside there's perfectionism,
But it's a lie,
For it only buries her strong desire
To accept her own humanity.

On the outside there are no cuts nor bruises,
But it's a lie,
For her smooth, unblemished skin only conceals
Massive internal wounds.

HUMPTY DUMPTY

The impact of that first betrayal
Shattered the clear crystal bubble of trust
That had provided my freedom to move and grow.
Scattered around me were millions of bits of glass,
Dangerously sharp and pointed,
But I knew that somehow,
With no help from the king's horses or the king's men,
I would have to put it back together again,
For I absolutely needed its protection just to survive.

Down on my bloody hands and knees
I gathered the splinters to me
And painstakingly pieced them together
Like a giant jigsaw puzzle.
The surfaces both inside and out were rough and uneven
With gaping cracks and unattractive scars,
A patchwork trust that seemed better than none.

Alternately then, again and again,
Betrayal smashed into my trust
And I worked feverishly to restore it,
Each time the bubble looking sorrier and sorrier
Until it offered no protection at all.
Finally I simply let the pieces lie
As I stood paralyzed by fear,
As aware as Eve of my nakedness,
Vulnerable and ashamed,
But with no recollection of ever having agreed
To taste the forbidden fruit.

ACTS OF TREASON

His enlistment, recorded on five certificates of birth,
Was perhaps, after all, impulsive,
But pledged he had
To serve and honor,
Protect and defend.
He performed his corporal duties
Toiling in the trenches, year in, year out,
The dullness of the routine
Sapping whatever idealism
Had induced him in the first place to join.
The sergeant barked out the orders
And he complied
More from weakness than commitment,
As he applied puny effort to rise in the ranks.
Emasculated and feeling powerless,
He saw his allegiance crumble
And his loyalty fall.
He betrayed those who depended on him for safety
And he inflicted them with wounds
In a futile attempt
To obliterate his own.
He received no recompense for his acts of treason
But the momentary illusion of being in command.
His actions were never disclosed,
So no formal charges were filed against him.

TERMS OF SURRENDER

My white flag droops limply on its staff,
Not enough pride left in it
To even attempt to flutter in the breeze,
Barely visible, but I know it is there
And so do you,
And we both know its meaning well.

Invisibly inscribed on my white flag
Are the non-negotiated terms of my surrender,
Tacitly agreed upon,
Unconditionally binding.

You will keep me physically alive,
And in return I will give to you my life
To do with as you will.
I will neither resist you nor wage battle against you;
I will guard the confidentiality of your movements;
I will restrain every impulse toward freedom;
I will inhibit every effort toward growth.

I will sleep-walk through this existence
Until the day that my white flag
Drapes your casket and accompanies you to the grave,
And then I will try to reclaim my life.

THE PUPPETEER

The puppeteer holds all the strings in his hands,
Strings attached to his Pinocchio-in-reverse,
His real live daughter turned into a wooden headed puppet.
The puppet's initial movement is awkward and jerky,
But soon she learns to subordinate her will to the puppeteer's,
And then she leaps and bounds and pirouettes and glides
And bows respectfully
At the slightest hint of his command.

The puppeteer in time wearies of this game
And turns his interest elsewhere,
Casually shoving the strings into his back pocket,
Dragging the puppet behind.
Her limbs are bent at odd angles as her fragile frame
Bounces, crashes, bumps, and scrapes
Along the hard, rough terrain.

After years of careless neglect
The tangle of strings succumbs to decay,
Releasing the girl at last from the puppeteer's passive control.
No matter; she has quite forgotten how
To exercise her will to cause free movement;
And the puppeteer waltzes away.

I'll Play Your Game

You write the rules
And you roll the dice.
You select my game piece for me
And you move it wherever you choose . . .
Three spaces forward,
Four spaces back.
You determine when I forfeit my turn;
You award my bonuses;
You assess my penalties.
I'll play your game with you,
Though I know you will always win.

SOMEWHERE ELSE

I'm really not here, you know.
I'm somewhere else far away
In a place where you can't find me.

It's my private underground paradise.
Soft velvet grass cushions my feet and sparkling crystals
Of pink and blue and yellow and violet
Light the ceiling high above my head.
Pure, cool water bubbles over smooth rounded stones.
The stream meanders downward
And falls over a twenty-five-foot ledge
Into an oval terraced pool where I love to swim.
Gentle deer come near me to drink
And cottontails nibble clover
And scamper among lilies and columbine.
Bluebirds twitter and swoop,
Streaming rose-colored ribbons behind them.

Though laden with precious gemstones and metals,
The value of this cavern lies only in its virgin beauty.
I will take nothing from it
And I will leave nothing behind.
It will always be my Somewhere Else
Where my mind and spirit can be free.

WHAT WILL HAPPEN?

What will happen to you
If someone finds out
What you are doing to me?
Will you lose your job?
Will neighbors point their fingers and stare?
Will the church excommunicate you?
Will you be carted off to jail?

What will happen to my mother
If she finds out
What you are doing to me?
Will she broken beyond repair?
Will she hate you?
Will she blame me?
Will she go away?

What will happen to my brother and sisters
If they find out
What you are doing to me?
Will they have to choose sides?
Will they embrace me or stone me?
Will they believe me?
Will they identify their experience with mine?

What will happen to me
If someone finds out what you are doing to me?
Will I be punished?
Will everyone hate me?
Will I be abandoned
And left to die?

Robyn Apffel

SOMEHOW I JUST KNEW

You never told me not to tell,
But somehow I just knew
That I had to keep this little activity
A secret between you and me.

Years before the word "clandestine"
Appeared on my vocabulary list,
I experienced its ugly meaning
And somehow I just knew that I must maintain full
    secrecy.

I was confused and frightened,
But somehow I just knew
That I had to bear all my burdens alone,
That I must hold all the pain inside me,
That I must never share my feelings with another soul.

The deed was done in darkness,
Hidden behind closed doors
With no witness to see.
You never needed to threaten me not to tell
Because somehow I just knew.

WHOM ARE YOU PROTECTING?

Why are you so afraid to tell?
Whom are you protecting anyway?
Your mother?
She's married to the man;
Surely she already knows what he is like.
It probably wouldn't surprise her, you know.
Do you think that she might throw him out
And that she can't afford to raise the family alone?
Do you think she has enough problems to deal with?
Do you think she doesn't notice that you're hurting?
She probably doesn't;
Her own pain clouds her eyes;
Perhaps a sound jolt would force her to open them.

Are you protecting your sisters?
Look at them carefully.
Are they smiling and self-assured?
Do they express a full range of feelings?
Do they look you straight in the eye?
Do you suppose he just might be doing the same to them,
Or do you believe him when he tells you
He does this with you because you are special?
Secrecy can't protect anyone;
Only the truth and the light of day can do that.

Perhaps you think you are protecting him.
You know how weak he is
And you try to be strong enough for the two of you;
But he is the parent and you are the child.
It is his job to protect you
And he is failing;
But it is his failure, not yours.
You should not have to protect him from the long
   reach of justice
Or your mother's wrath or public humiliation.
You should not have to protect him from his own
   weakness.

Are you protecting yourself?
Are you afraid that exposure will damage your
   reputation?
Are you afraid that no one will believe you?
You are vulnerable and totally dependent
And you know you need your parents to take care
   of you.
You must be so frightened of being left alone.
You probably even believe
That this utter disrespect for your person
Is the price that you must pay for survival;
But you would be dead wrong.

WHERE IS YOUR BABY DOLL?

Where is your baby doll, Child?
You had her with you this morning
When you went off to play.
She was sitting right there in the red wagon
That you pulled along behind you
With the tartan plaid blanket and a picnic lunch
For you and your Daddy.
Where is your baby doll now?

I left her at the playground, Mom.
She needs to run and play,
Build castles in the sandbox,
Swing high enough to touch the sky,
Climb and hang upside-down on the monkey bars,
Get dizzy on the merry-go-round,
Zoom down the steepest slide,
Engineer the big wooden train.
She needs to jump rope
And hopscotch with her friends;
She needs to drink gallons of soda pop
And spoil her appetite with gobs of cotton candy.
She needs to fashion crowns of daisies
And chase after monarch butterflies,
Catch slimy green frogs,
And follow caterpillar trails.

I left her at the playground, Mom,
So she can do all the things
A little girl needs to do to grow.

Using Writing Prompts

At the end of each chapter, you will find writing prompts to help transition from my story to your own. Each prompt will begin by asking you to re-read one of the poems from the chapter, followed by some questions to get you thinking about how your own experience compares to mine. Sometimes you might say, "Yes, that's exactly what happened to me!" but usually there will be marked differences between your experience and mine, and even if the experience happens to be the same or very similar, your response to it will surely be unique.

You will be directed to write your own poem based on the feelings brought forth from reading mine. Always your experience, your feelings, and your words will be far more important and more legitimate for you than anything I may have written. You may wish to imitate my style of a particular poem, or you may choose to express yourself in your own creative manner; whichever you choose, make it an authentic choice. If something I have said makes you angry, write that anger; if it makes you sad, write that sadness; if it makes you laugh, write something funny. The whole point of the writing prompts is to tap into your emotions and to commit your emotions to paper.

I have selected for writing prompts the poems that had something important to say to me. You certainly don't have to do any or all of the writing prompts as I have presented them. Choose the poems or topics that have the most meaning to you. My suggestions are just that: suggestions. Use them in a way that best serves you.

Writing Prompts for Part I, The Early Years, Accountability

1. Re-read "Don't Be Afraid." Who were you afraid of? How and how often were you left alone in the care of your abuser? Was anyone else aware that you were afraid of this person? Write your own poem about your fear.
2. Re-read "Daddy." What did you call your abuser, Daddy, Grandpa, Uncle Joe? What should your relationship with this person have been like? What was it like instead? Write your own poem calling your abuser by name.
3. Re-read "Train Track Lives." Were any of your siblings also abused? Do you even know for sure? Did you ever talk to your siblings about your abuse? Were you and your siblings allies or rivals during your childhood? Write your own poem about your relationship with one or more of your siblings.
4. Re-read "Magic Touch." How did your abuser take advantage of your youth and innocence? What lies did your abuser tell you that you thought at the time were true? When and how did you recognize betrayal? Write your own poem that explores the trickery used by your abuser against you.
5. Re-read "Humpty Dumpty." How did you try to protect yourself from your abuser? Did you blame yourself for the abuse? How long did the abuse go on? Write your own poem about measures you took to protect yourself from your abuser and the

effectiveness of your efforts, remembering that you were a child and your abuser was an adult.

6. Re-read "What Will Happen?" Explore your own sense of responsibility for other people close to you, including your abuser. How did you feel responsible to protect others? How did you think you could live with being blamed for the consequences to the family if the abuse had been discovered? Write your own poem about how you thought your abuse might have affected others.

PART II

TWELVE TO TWENTY, DEVELOPING SURVIVAL STRATEGIES

Robyn Apffel

Adolescence is difficult at best, for both the teenager and the rest of the world. As the youngest of five children I had already witnessed the turmoil of the twelve to twenty set years before I arrived there myself. I had already experienced four years of sexual abuse by the time I turned twelve and had learned to take whatever came my way and cope with it as best as I could. My survival strategies were firmly in place . . . don't ask any questions . . . don't tell any secrets . . . keep the mask on at all costs. At the time in my life when I should have been developing social skills and discovering myself separate from my parents, I went into hiding. As far as I was concerned, the key to my survival rested in denying my own existence, for no one could harm what did not exist.

Even the physical changes my body was undergoing did not move me to inquire. I had my first menstrual period at the age of ten, and I believed that I was dying, and I merely accepted it. I was surprised when it stopped and puzzled when it started again, stopped again, started again, stopped again. Around the third time my mother picked up that my menses had begun and had a confrontation with me about blood on my underpants. She never explained to me what it was, only where she kept the pads and how to put one on. I don't think she asked if I had any questions, but even if she had, I would not have asked. A year later when they were showing the traditional film to fifth grade girls at school, I can remember my parents discussing whether or not Robyn should see it, finally agreeing to sign the damn permission slip. I sat in the auditorium, but I didn't listen to any of the information on the film. I suppose my curiosity had been killed by the overriding conviction that I really shouldn't be finding out whatever was in that movie. And that was how I approached all of the changes my body went through . . . I denied that it was happening, and continued to see myself as a child, without developed breasts, with no hair growth on private parts of my body, baby smooth skin, no womanly pride.

We had no full-length mirrors in the house, and even if we had I doubt that I would have stood naked in front of one. I did use make-up, lipstick by the time I was in eighth grade, and in high school the full complement of eye shadow, liner, mascara, and I curled my hair. I thought I was rather pretty. My features were attractive enough . . . a nicely shaped face, pretty eyes, an ordinary nose which was about as good as noses get, good coloring, and a lovely smile. I was big for my age, the tallest girl in my class until I reached the eighth grade, when someone taller moved into the district. I believed the other kids when they called me fat, but when I look at my pictures from those years, I realize that I was certainly not fat then, just slightly overweight.

I hated my clothes, mostly hand-me-down or hand-made, and rarely of my choosing. I loved very feminine dresses, but owned none. Perhaps they were too expensive or impractical. More likely, feminine was not my mother's taste, and she selected all my clothes until I was in college. Once in college, I lost weight and either bought or made very feminine clothes for myself. I developed a passion for silk, satin, lace, and velvet, and preferred pastels and flowered prints to the brightly colored stripes or geometric patterns that were all the fashion of the mid-1960's. Still, it surprised me when friends would use the word "feminine" to describe me; to me, that was my ideal, something I dreamed of being, but would never attain.

My most difficult years were between grades five and eight because those were the most active years of the sexual abuse and the most painful for me socially. Until fifth grade I had gotten along well with nearly all my classmates, but suddenly I found myself being ostracized at the very time I most needed peer support. Kids seem to sense vulnerability and they test it to the utmost. My balancing act was so incredibly delicate; I opted for the adult acceptance of my teachers and sacrificed peer relationships. I had a few good friends, and they really were good, reliable friends. I probably could have confided in them what was happening to me at home, but I didn't know how to share intimate secrets, and I'm not even sure that I knew the abuse was something that should have been disclosed in those years long before "Good Touch/Bad Touch" and "Stranger Danger."

School was my haven, and was the only place I had felt truly safe. I spent as much time there as I possibly could, joining every club available and participating in activities that would get me home after everyone else had arrived home from work or school in the early evening. I developed friendships with several teachers and was pleased to be treated with respect by the very people I held in such high esteem. They taught me much about life, love, and generosity. It is little wonder that I decided to become a teacher.

I came very close once to telling one of my teachers about my home situation, but for the most part I learned to protect myself by avoiding being home. Meanwhile, I developed an interest in young men. I liked boys and had a series of boyfriends from the time I entered high school until the day I got engaged. I was highly selective about whom I dated, and made very few errors in judgment. My relationships were sweet and innocent and I liked it that way. It never occurred to me to question the young man's reason for not pressuring me for sex; I presumed that he was being respectful of me. Years later, my therapist suggested that perhaps the young men I had consistently selected had some sexual issues of their own! Interesting! I find it rather amusing that during my teen years my mother warned me never to be alone in the house with one of my boyfriends, without ever elaborating on why. I would have been safe with any one of them. She should have told me never to be alone in the house with my father.

Innocence was as important to me as femininity, and although my body had been corrupted over and over again, my mind retained its innocence, as a matter of fact, for too many years, well into my adulthood. So determined was I to reclaim my innocence that I held onto it to the point of delusion. I was forty years old before I happily participated in the sexual act with my husband to whom I had already been married for eighteen years. It's easy to see how it happened. My father had taken me against my will; I recognized that fact when I was sixteen years old, and although I did not confront the reality of the abuse until many years later, I believed with all my mind that I could take control of my life and make it whatever I wanted it to be, regardless of my inexperience with life.

The most serious intrusion on my adolescence caused by the abuse was the interference with my developing social skills. I had great confidence in my ability to do, but none in my capacity to be. I was academically strong, artistic, creative, and even rather athletic. Although I loved music, I turned my back on it because my father was musically talented. I also avoided writing, other than for assignments, even though many people told me I was gifted writer, because my father also wrote. I was determined to be myself, different from my mother, my father, my sisters, my brother; I had no idea how much of my true self I was denying by not permitting myself to enjoy or participate in any activity that reminded me of my family. As far as I was concerned, being myself meant not being like them.

Still, I was not at all a rebellious teenager. I was a child of the sixties, and by the time I was in college, my parents had moved across the country and I really was totally on my own, except for financially. I have never used drugs nor even tried a cigarette, and although I have tasted alcohol, I much prefer chocolate. Sometimes even today when I refuse alcohol, someone will comment on my virtue. "Virtue," I tell them, "has nothing to do with it. I just don't like alcohol, the way it tastes or the way it makes me feel. When I say no to a hot fudge sundae, now, that is virtue." I have lived an extraordinarily straight life, and I'm not really sure why I never experimented with the wild side of life when I certainly had the opportunity to do so. I'm not saying that I regret those particular choices, but I do realize now that my teenage years were not at all a time of growth for me. Most of my energy during the years when I should have been learning independence was devoted to holding onto what tiny shred of innocence I could grasp. Since I did not learn independence, it has been difficult for me to learn interdependence, and because my every thought was on self-protection, I struggle still with becoming less self-centered. Growing up is hard at fourteen; it's no easier at forty, especially when everyone expects that you've already done it. When pretense has become a way of life, authenticity is almost unthinkable.

The poems in this chapter present a young woman who seems to have her act very much together, and I did seem to do that. Appearances can be very deceiving, though it is true that we often grow into the masks that we wear. I made lots of good choices throughout my adolescence and into adulthood, so I don't really question my choices. What I do question is my motivation. If I had decided to be Goody-Two-Shoes out of a strong conviction that being good is right, I would feel satisfied now with my actions, but my motivation was not conviction; it was fear. I had nothing together. I was afraid of life, all of it; I was afraid of people, I was afraid of my own bodily sensations, I was afraid of God, I was afraid of both living and dying. I was afraid of the incomprehensible and unpredictable reality, but no one would ever see my fear. I knew by the age of ten how to act out a script so that I would never have to deal with my fears of reality because what I was living was unreal. By the very end of this chapter, I have finally come to the realization that I needed to take some control of my life and that I did, indeed, have the power to do so.

WHAT DO YOU THINK?

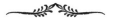

Do you think we ought to tell her
How her body will change
As she becomes a woman?
Do you think she needs to know?

Do you think she's even noticed
How her sisters all have grown?
Do you think she looks at them
And wonders when the same will happen to her?

She never asks any questions;
She's so quiet and withdrawn.
At times I'm sure she's totally oblivious
And at others I'd swear she already knows.

How could she know about womanhood?
She and I aren't exactly close
And I've never told her what to expect
About her own sexuality or about men.

What do you think?
Would it be better for you to tell her?
Would it be better if she hears it from a man?
Thank God! If you do it, I won't have to.

MY BODY

I'd like to divorce my body,
Just step outside of it
And walk away.
I don't love it any more.
We used to get along just fine,
My body and I.
We used to have great fun together
Running freely and dancing wildly,
Embracing the joy of life, delightful.
But lately,
We can't seem to agree on anything.
I wish to remain a child,
But my body keeps growing,
Evolving into a woman.
I long to cling to my innocence
But my body leaps boldly into maturity.
My body has feelings of its own,
Feelings that I don't share,
Feelings that frighten me.
I just can't trust my body any more.
The very sight of it sickens me.
I want this relationship to end.

BODY, MIND, SPIRIT

I deny this body;
I want no part of it;
It does not belong to me.

My mind I accept.
My mind is free
And cannot be used
Or controlled by others.
My mind protects me
And comforts me
And encourages me to persevere.
My mind speaks to me truthfully
And provides images and words
That I can believe and hold onto.

I hate this body;
I want to disown it;
It causes me pain.

My spirit I love.
My spirit is beautiful;
It keeps me alive.
It is kind and gentle
And even forgiving.
My spirit is a gift from God
And is the part of me that comprehends God.
I am certain that my spirit
Is more precious than gold.

I am afraid of this body;
It deceives me;
It tells me that I have no value.

IT OUGHT TO HURT

Why doesn't it hurt when you touch me?
Your rough hands rub my delicate flesh
And I expect to feel pain,
But instead I feel warmth and pleasure
And I don't understand.

It ought to hurt when you bite my ear,
When your teeth clasp my lobe
And your hot breath blasts
Uninvited into my ear canal,
But it tickles and makes me shiver.

Your fondling ought to repel me,
But my breasts receive it as a caress,
Sweet and exciting,
And I tingle from the roots of my hair
To the tips of my toes.

Your fiery tongue ought to burn my lips
And your unwelcome kiss ought to suffocate me.
The weight of your body on top of mine
Ought to crush all the life out of me.
"It ought to hurt," I cry. "It ought to hurt!"

Robyn Apffel

MIRROR, MIRROR

Profound black-bottomed pool
Undisturbed surface reflecting
Lengths of light full spectrum image
Through aqueous humor then lens
Striking retinal receptors

Optic cables transmit information
Cerebrum decodes acceptable countenance
Lovable enough as Narcissus
Emotions override intelligence:
Reject despise her likeness to her father

SCHOOL DAYS

Nine to three,
One-hundred-eighty days a year,
September through June,
Kindergarten through high school.
Books, pencils, crayons, tempera paints,
Chalkboards, erasers, milk money and ice cream bars.

Predictability . . .
Knowing what behavior induces a smile,
What action effects a scolding;
Spelling tests on Fridays,
Gym class on Tuesdays and Thursdays,
Music on Mondays from two till three.

Orderliness . . .
Desks and chairs in five rows of five,
Coat and hat go on this hook,
Homework goes here,
Paste goes there,
Clean up all scraps of paper before you leave.

Fairness . . .
All materials belong to all and must be shared;
Everyone gets a chance to lead the flag salute,
Collect the lunch money,
Carry messages to the office,
Be team captain.

Discipline . . .
A teaching of what is right
By modeling and explanation;
With expectation of compliance
And reasonable consequences for infractions;
Taught with love and respect.

What happens the rest of the time?
Three to nine,
One-hundred-eighty-five days a year,
July and August,
Birth to kindergarten and beyond high school
    graduation . . .
What happens then?

LA HABANA

La Habana enfolds all ships large and small,
Domestic, foreign, battered, elegant,
Equally offering shelter to all,
Guaranteeing safety from the unpredictable sea.

La Habana simulates ocean's waves and currents
In dress rehearsal on a spiraling scale,
Fairy tale simplicity for little tugs,
Approaching reality for huge ocean liners.

La Habana opens her arms to welcome all
And teaches skills of navigation,
Gently guiding, coaxing, challenging,
Daring her charges to venture forth.

La Habana opens her arms to release all
Who have grown and earned their sea-legs
In the protection of her tender care,
Who are now prepared for the open sea.

TEACHER'S PET

So eager to please that she forgets
Other children are watching and judging her every move
As she volunteers for each unpleasant task
Just to reap the attention, approval, acceptance
Of the only adult in her classroom, her teacher.

The youngest child of five, unplanned,
Keenly aware of the financial burden her life represents,
Inexplicably battered in spite of her best efforts
To do what is right and to be perfect,
She is now bewildered by her father's sexual advances.

She is perceptive enough to have discerned
That in school she can find the support that is absent at home,
Simply by doing what is expected of her
And by doing it just a little bit better than anyone else,
By going just an extra half-mile.

What escapes her notice is the price she must pay
For the adult approval she so desperately seeks.
For a pat on the back, a kind word, and a smile,
She unknowingly forfeits friendships, social ease,
Peer acceptance, and a place where she truly belongs.

A Fine Family

Ah, so you think I come
From a fine family, do you?
Well, I guess it must be true . . .
You're smart . . . you're my teacher . . .
And me? I'm just a kid,
So what do I know?

A fine family . . .
Well, I'll tell you one thing . . .
We're not at all like "Father Knows Best."
But, okay, that's just TV,
Some made-up ideal
That never happens in real life.

But what exactly do you mean by
"A fine family"?
Is my perception of reality
So different from yours?
Or perhaps you don't even know
What my reality is.

What do you really know
About my family anyway?
Let's see: you know my brother;
You know my sisters; and you know me.
Hmmm. You're right . . .
I do come from a fine family.

THE OBSERVER

Separated from the crowd
By distance and by intent
She retreats into the deep shadows
From where she monitors minutely
The faces, the actions, the words, the feelings
Of those who dance before her,
Oblivious to her inspection.

She studies their masks of fine porcelain,
Smooth and flawless, painted to perfection,
But hard and cool to the touch;
Unfeeling and changeless; lovely, but quite unreal.
And gladly would she trade her tear-streaked reality
For the radiance of a bogus smile.

She observes their fluid motions,
Steeped in the confidence
Of those having graduated
Madame Sousseuax's finishing school,
Knowing for certain the right things to do;
And she camouflages her own insecurity
In the sanctuary of risk-free immobility.

She assimilates every uttered sound,
The meaningless chatter
And the highly significant laughter;
She reads skillfully between the lines,
Gathering megabytes of social information
That she analyzes, sorts, and files for future recall,
But from which she shrinks to practice.

She penetrates deceptively veiled emotions:
The uncertainty of lustful, hopeful young men;
The smoldering desires of pseudo-modest young ladies;
She witnesses the interactions between them,
Both apprehensive, both feigning courage.
She knows the ambivalence of yearning to connect
While refusing to chance rejection or betrayal.

She notices everything and everybody
And scrutinizes them in great detail;
She grasps all that she sees
She comprehends all that she hears;
She remembers all that she surveys.
She watches as life waltzes by,
But she is only an observer, and she does not dance.

Robyn Apffel

CLIQUES AND NICHES

Monochromatic threads tightly woven cloth
Blanket bound edge-stitched
In uniform tensile twist
Even straight flat squared
Resistant to fraying
Undecorated color-free
Stain-repellant muslin

They march like soldiers blue
On a field of green
An exclusive clique
Shiny black boots
Polished brass buttons
Snow white cotton gloves
Defending their position of power

Variegated fibers loosely woven gauze
Pinked and unbound
In unique delicate silk
Crazy-quilt patchwork puckered rough
Open to use and tear
Richly embroidered sequined and trimmed
Stain-absorbent voile

She hides like a bashful violet
In a garden of towering lilies
A cozy niche
Pink satin slippers
Rose velvet ribbons
Plumed purple bonnet
Seeking refuge in a forgotten corner

Robyn Apffel

A FEW GOOD FRIENDS

The soulful ones are they,
My friends, those few most special people
Who see beyond my figure and face,
Who know beneath my actions and speech,
Who feel deeply into the goodness of my heart.

From them I cannot hide
The most tender parts of my being
That I have tried oh so carefully to protect,
That I have learned so fully to deny,
That I myself have quite forgotten even exist.

They are magicians and fortunetellers
Who are not bound by limits of vision,
Who clearly hear my inaudible cries
And touch me, soul to soul,
Understanding to understanding.

They are my few good friends who know and accept me
And allow me the great precious freedom
To be and to grow and to love them
And to reveal to them the beauty of my spirit
That I keep hidden from everyone else.

SEVEN O'CLOCK IN THE MORNING

It's seven o'clock in the morning!
Who could be knocking at our door?
It must be Robyn; who else would it be?
Doesn't that girl have a home of her own?

Susan! Sandy! Robyn's here.
Open the door and let her in.
See if she needs something for breakfast,
Then get ready for school.

Every morning! Why does she come by so early?
It's almost as if she wants to get away
From something that's happening
At her own house. But what?

Oh, I hear rumors about loud fighting,
Rumors about her old man
Running around with other women,
Rumors about beatings and slamming of doors.

Robyn has never said anything about it
To me or to our daughters.
She always acts like everything is okay,
A little shy, perhaps, but otherwise pretty normal.

She does seem a little afraid of you, Tom,
Though I know you've never hurt her in any way.
She never talks to you or even looks at you,
But she's comfortable enough with me.

Oh, well, there's nothing we can do
Unless she asks us for help.
Maybe nothing is wrong.
Rumors are often false, you know.

I guess it's not so bad that she comes
At seven o'clock in the morning.
We have to get up anyway
And get ready for work and the kids off to school.

AT THE BUS STOP

I can wait for the school bus at the corner of Elmwood
    and Main,
Just a minute-and-a-half walk from my front door;
Get on the bus at seven-twenty-two.
Or I can walk down to Sunrise Street
To catch the bus there at seven-o-five;
It'll take me twenty minutes to get there
If I go the long way around. Sounds good to me!
That'll get me out of the house at six-forty-five.
He never gets back home that early.

What a way to start every morning before I go to school!
I always have to find a way to get out of this house.
I wonder how many times he's come home now
After dropping Mom off at work,
Expecting to find me home, but I'm gone.
Why did it take me so long to wise up?
I used to just sit and wait
And sometimes he would come and sometimes not,
But it always felt the same to me: terrifying.

I wonder how he does it! Doesn't he have to be at work?
It's half an hour round trip,
Plus the fifteen minutes or so he spends molesting me.
Seems like a lot of trouble to go to
For that quarter hour of pleasure, his not mine.
You'd think someone would find out and put a stop to this.
Well, I'm going to put a stop to it!
I just won't be here when he comes back home.
Sooner or later he'll figure it out and stop this nonsense.
Then I'll be able to wait at my own bus stop.

ON GUARD

I watch standing sentry,
Alert, ever vigilant, ready,
Expecting my assailant's approach.
There is no sign of his presence now,
But I know he is very clever
And may appear at any instant
From out of nowhere,
And I must be prepared.

In this silence my ears can detect
The softest whisper,
The slightest creak.
I know the sound of his movements;
His timing may be unpredictable
But his habits are firmly fixed.
So I listen every moment
For the trumpet to announce his return.

It could be days until he arrives
Or even months;
I never know
So I must always be on guard
Every second of every day
Just in case the time is now.
There is nothing I can do to stop him,
But at least I will know he is coming.

BOXED

These walls close so tight around me,
Cramping my shoulders
And pressing down on my head,
Stifling the claustrophobic breath
I have recycled a thousand times.

This box binds me like tiny Chinese feet
That have been denied the freedom
To run and to grow,
Holding me in a frozen state
Of emotional immaturity.

My eyes encounter only darkness
Inside this prison from which there is no escape.
I can pound and holler and scream my head off
But no one will hear me
Outside this soundproofed vault.

How in the world did this happen?
I am dying in here and I can't even remember
Whether someone incarcerated me
Or I, in some misguided effort at self-protection,
Fashioned this cell around myself.

EMOTIONAL ARMOR

She's just a little more than a child
Unable to defend against the wit,
The will, and the wiles of a man
She ought to be able to trust.

Her arms can't protect her
From his strength turned against her.
She can't run fast enough or far enough
To escape his powerful reach.

She can't stay hidden forever;
He always finds her sooner or later,
And when he does he will punish her
For denying him his pleasure.

Better to put on emotional armor
That will keep her safe
Even as he performs his terrible deeds,
Even as her body suffers harm.

Her emotional armor keeps him at a distance,
And the beauty of it,
The sheer beauty of it!
Is that he doesn't even know it.

He thinks he has her, body and soul!
But she has fled his evil grasp.
She is out to lunch,
And he doesn't even know it.

HOLD ME, PLEASE

I'm seventeen years old now . . .
I've already been through a few serious boyfriends
And have a new one right now,
A football player, member of the National Honor Society,
His Dad's a drunk, but he won't follow in those footsteps.
I wonder if he'll ever kiss me;
If he does, I'll be his first.
I wish I could talk to him
And tell him what's happening in my life.
I wish he would just hold me until the pain goes away.

All my friends and my teachers have been worried about me.
The last four days I've done nothing but cry.
They say it's not like me,
I'm usually so happy, so up.
I'm so tired of the pretense.
They send me to my guidance counselor.
He's okay, I guess, to help with scheduling,
To help with college applications,
But I don't want to talk to him about my problems;
I don't want him to hold me.

Is there someone I would talk to, he asks me;
It's really obvious that I need help.
Yes, there is one person I trust,
My Ancient History teacher;
He'll be a guidance counselor himself one day;
Yeah, I can talk to him.
So we meet in the guidance office,
And I want desperately to tell him my story;
I want to tell him so he can help me deal with it;
I want him to hold me, just hold me.

I try to speak, but the words are jumbled in my brain
And they won't come out of my mouth.
As tears begin to flow, I feel embarrassed,
And I wonder how to get out of this.
I don't know what to say,
So I just reach up and throw my arms around his neck
And I hold on tight, so very tight.
In an instant reflex motion,
He pushes me away, not unkindly, but firmly,
And now he is embarrassed.

I apologize to him and he says it's okay,
He understands that sometimes we all need to reach out,
But he doesn't offer to hold me,
And he still has no idea what I had wanted to tell him.
I pull myself together and stop crying
And manage somehow to get through the rest of my senior
    year,
Happy, smiling, always up.
Eventually my boyfriend does give me that kiss,
And it is all very sweet and innocent, just the way I like it.
But I still need someone to hold me.

FLY AWAY

Fly away, Robin,
Fly to a warmer place
Where sunshine and sustenance
Are within your grasp.

Leave this nest;
It provides you no shelter;
It offers you no home;
There is nothing here to hold you.

Fly away to safety.
Find yourself a harbor;
Accept its protection;
Receive its care.

You do have a choice, Robin;
You can leave this place
Any time you wish.
So fly away, fly, fly away!

"I can't," replies Robin.
"My feet are tethered,
My wings are clipped,
And I don't know how to fly."

INNOCENCE RETAINED

He has had his filthy hands all over her,
He has defiled her body and snatched away her virginity;
He has implicated her in his rutting behavior.
He has distorted her perception of love and trust,
And has thoroughly muddied her emotional state.
He has confounded her mind and has tried to
    convince her
That she is guilty of his sin.

Now on the brink of young womanhood
She stands by a wholesome, inexperienced man,
He as innocent of body as she is of spirit.
Their desire is for love, sweetness, and purity.
Their gifts to each other
Are friendship, security, comfort, and peace.
They walk together in trust, unafraid.

She leads the double life, not by her choosing.
In private, she succumbs to her father's will,
Helpless to defend against his unwelcome corruption.
She surrenders her body to his power
While her emotions flee to safety,
Denying the reality that she is forced to endure.
In private, she yields to incest just to survive.

In public, she appears the freshest virgin,
Angelic and immaculate, completely naïve.
To her it is not pretense, but the reality that
    defines her.
Her father may have raped her body;
He may have ravaged her emotions;
But he has utterly failed to plunder her soul.
Her soul is the guardian of her innocence.

IN HIS HANDS

How can I trust any man
After my own father has abused me so?
Why would I even want
To love a man and to have a man love me?
But I do; I do!

I like men! It's sex I want to avoid!
I don't want to wrestle
In the back seat of a car
Needing constantly to defend myself
Against unwanted fondling.

I treasure soft kisses and firm embraces,
Walking together holding hands,
Whispering and endlessly sharing secrets,
Supporting and encouraging each other,
A masculine balance to my femininity.

I love a man who has the strength
To take control of his own emotions
And to assume the lead
That nurtures my growth
While respecting my need for protection.

My judgment is sound.
I will place myself willingly
In the hands of a man who loves my soul;
Him I will trust completely
To keep me safe and do me no harm.

THE SWEETHEART TREE

Ah! What unfortunate beech tree
Chosen on account of its thin, smooth skin,
So easily carved into with a dull, rusty blade;
A heart pierced by a rising arrow,
P.J. + K.M. 4 ever,
Sealed with a kiss beneath April's shower.

The Sweetheart Tree spangled
With bold declarations of evergreen intentions,
Dear testimonials deep in passion
But shallow in durability,
As fleeting as the deciduous parasol
That proffers shade from summer's sun.

Through a century of seasons it stands
Bearing the graffiti of the generations
Telling lies that once were true,
Revealing shared-in-whispers dreams
Of youth's compelling desire for eternity,
Now stripped and exposed to October's frost.

Ancient and weary at last it falls,
Its messages meaningless scars
Of broken hearts and forgotten promises.
A woodsman wielding axe and wedge
Chops and splits and stacks the cords
To burn, intense burning love, to vanquish winter's chill.

I Don't Know Anything About That

Other girls ask me because they think I must know
About intercourse, pregnancy, and feminine needs,
But I don't know anything about that.

You can ask me about history and literature,
Science, mathematics, and especially grammar . . .
I can tell you all about those things.
I can speak to you in three different languages
And recite the Prologue to the Canterbury Tales in Olde
    English.
I've memorized algebraic equations and chemical formulas
And I can tell you the details of trivial historical events.
My mind is open to various opinions
Of philosophy, psychology, and theology.
I delight in intellectual challenge
And I am very comfortable with paradox.

But don't ask me anything about sex;
I closed my mind to that subject years ago
And I honestly don't know anything about it.

BORDER PATROL

Actively recruited by the highly selective service,
He willingly performs his duty
Of guarding her personal boundaries.
She herself is a conscientious objector,
So shell-shocked from having spent her life in a war
    zone
That she refuses to defend her own position
And relies instead on the enlisted men
Who volunteer for the special forces of sentry detail.

His tour of duty begins with reconnaissance,
Laboring through her obstacle course
To determine the perimeter of her territory.
His mission is to resist all encroachment
And to establish an impenetrable stronghold
From which to operate his command.
His assignment is to relentlessly patrol her borders
And to safeguard the vulnerability of her post.

If he successfully fulfills his commission
She will urge him to reenlist with promotion for
    another hitch.
She will award him a Medal of Honor
And the Distinguished Service Cross.
He may even accept her invitation to become a lifer
Who will continue to discharge his sentry duties
Until such service is no longer required;
Then he will retire with full pay and benefits.

Robyn Apffel

GREAT NEW WORLD

He: Take my hand, my Turtledove,
     Come walk with me, explore
     This great new world, a virgin land,
     We've never seen before.

     Up and down the mountainsides
     Blazing our own fresh trails,
     We'll tumble down sheer waterfalls
     Into deeply-shadowed vales.

     We'll taste the honeysuckle,
     Inhale perfume of rose,
     Quench our thirst with sweet red wine
     That through the canyon flows.

     We'll kiss the warmth of springtime;
     We'll flame like summer's sun;
     We'll cocoon together in autumn;
     And emerge when winter's done.

     So take my hand, my Turtledove,
     Come walk with me, explore
     This great new world, a virgin land
     We've never seen before.

She: *I'll take your hand, but stay with me*
           Right here, right where we are.
           The mountains are too steep for me,
           The valleys much too far.

           The trails are strewn with boulders
           And conifers fallen down;
           The rapids are so treacherous
           I'm certain we will drown.

           The honeysuckle's dry as sand;
           The rose has lost its bloom;
           The wine, it tastes of bitterness;
           The canyon is a tomb.

           Summer's heat will scorch us;
           Winter's ice will kill;
           Spring will just deceive us;
           And autumn will only chill.

           Let's stay right here forever, Dear;
           That world's not new to me.
           I've been across that land and back
           And there's nothing I care to see.

Robyn Apffel

DAISY WON'T TELL

Daisy flourishes in her own patch of sunshine,
A golden smile among the thorns.
She knows much more than she'll ever tell
Of anguish, injury, suffering, pain.

Daisy stretches to reach the clouds
And enfolds herself in their softness,
Cool and misty cumulus
Insulating her from unwanted memories.

Daisy turns her palms sunward
And photosynthesizes
All her goodness, decency, and beauty,
Nourishment for her own survival.

Daisy sinks her roots deep into hard, anemic soil
Holding tight to her innocence
Through tempest and hailstorm,
Through drought's parching flame.

Daisy won't tell you where she has been.
From seed to flower she has grown
Overcoming the hostile environment
That her loveliness disclaims.

PUT DOWN THE PEN AND TURN OFF THE MUSIC

I write:
Letters and poetry.
And as much as I revel in the creativity
I delight in the physical process as well
Penmanship
Forming perfect letters
Round o's
Tall t's straight at a seventy-five degree angle
F's that dip
As far below the line as they rise above
Fine black script on smooth white vellum.
But he writes, so I put down my pen.

I sing:
Hymns and popular tunes.
I sing mostly on key soprano melody
With an average range
Surely amateur
But with commitment and enthusiasm
Joyful
Singing the words of pure poetry
Soft and lovely
Sounds of meaning to the accompaniment
Of flute and piano, trumpet and violin.
But he sings, so I turn off the music.

GUILTY AS CHARGED

The judge proclaimed me, "Guilty as charged,"
Without benefit of a fair trial
Based upon the testimony of a sole witness,
The one who had framed me.
And then she pronounced my sentence:
To carry the weight of my skates that night
As my older brother and sisters,
Including the one who had framed me,
Had fun on the ice,
And I, just ten years old then, was to watch.

I didn't flinch when my sentence was passed
For I knew that the judge
Would not be at the frozen lake to view my execution;
She stayed at home, warm and cozy,
Leaving the bailiff to carry out my punishment.
And I knew him
And I was confident that he would believe me;
After all, I was telling the truth.
I was certain that because of our special relationship
He, at least, would believe me.

And it really didn't concern me
That he was powerless to commute my sentence.
I would serve my term with no complaint;
God knows I'd done that many times before.
All that mattered to me was that he believe me.
With all their skates laced up and tied now,
My brother and sisters gleefully glided onto the ice.
As he and I walked, his arm tight around me,
Beyond the trees and into the dark night,
I proclaimed to him my innocence.

"We know you did it," was all he said
As he proceeded to remove my coat, my sweater, my blouse.
He touched me as he had touched me so many times before,
Only this time it felt very different.
It was cold, freezing cold,
In the dark away from the floodlights of the rink,
But I knew clearly for the first time in my life
That what he was doing had nothing at all to do with me;
I wasn't special to him; he didn't believe me.
I was innocent, but he didn't give a damn about me.

TWENTY/TWENTY

Blurred by lenses unsuited to my eyes
But fitted precisely to yours,
My vision was impaired, distorted,
Miscomprehending form and feature,
Misinterpreting action and intent.

Artificial light was never quite bright enough
To illuminate your face so I could see
The myriad lines and creases,
Blemishes and scars of wounds
That you so meticulously concealed.

But then in a brief unguarded moment,
Your movement, usually so calculated, satin smooth,
Clumsily knocked the spectacles
From before my eyes,
Revealing to me the ungarnished truth.

At twenty feet my naked eyes focused upon
Minuscule details and tiny flaws
I recognized at once as lies and abuse.
I saw you divested of all glamor and pretense,
Human, culpable, and small.

And I think I could have accepted that reality;
I think I might have understood, even forgiven;
But in panic you shoved the glasses
Back onto my face, hoping that I would forget
What my eyes had clearly seen.

So I learned to be ashamed of my imperfections.
I learned to cover, flee, and deny,
And pretend that any one of us
Can aspire to the perfection of divinity;
And if we can't achieve it, then we must fake it.

But still I harbor the memory
Of seeing your humanity exposed,
And I pray that some day I will have the courage
To move towards the very attainable goals
Of openness, honesty, forgiveness, and love.

AT THE TOP OF THE STAIRS

I stepped out of my dressing room
And onto the stage at the top of the stairs.
Curtain time: same play, same scene.
I had memorized all my lines,
But I did not want to recite them.

He thought I'd missed my cue
When I would not respond
To his dramatic declaration of love;
He acted as if I were confused
When I turned away from his kiss.

I altered every stage direction
And rewrote the entire dialogue of his script.
Inspired by my successful improvisation,
I plotted to push him backwards down the stairs,
But my character would never commit such an action.

I was unaware of it then, but he realized
That I had assumed the role of the playwright
That day at the top of the stairs,
Empowered by my refusal to perform his scenario
And by my insistence upon playing my own part.

Writing Prompts for Part II: Twelve to Twenty, Developing Survival Strategies

1. Re-read "My Body." How do you feel about your body? How did your feelings about your body change after the abuse began? How does your body image affect your acceptance of your gender? Write your own poem exploring your relationship to your own body.

2. Re-read "It Ought to Hurt." How did you feel emotionally during abuse? How did you feel physically? Explore the conflict, if there was one, and write a poem about it.

3. Re-read "La Habana." What was your haven during the time you were abused? Who were the people who made you feel safe? Reflect on how the kindness, caring, and love of individuals gave you the strength to survive the abuse and write about it.

4. Re-read "Emotional Armor." Although you were unable to protect your body, you probably developed strategies to protect your emotional and spiritual states. Write about those strategies.

5. Re-read "Hold Me, Please." What, specifically, would have given you comfort that you were too afraid to ask for? Do you still yearn for that comfort? Has there been someone in your life you trusted enough to fulfill your need for comfort? Write a poem about your experience of seeking physical or emotional comfort.

6. Re-read "Put Down the Pen and Turn Off the Music." In what ways have you identified with

your abuser? Do you look like him/her? Do you share similar interests or talents? How do the similarities make you feel? Write a poem about that.

7. Re-read "At the Top of the Stairs." Do you remember a time when you actively resisted attempted abuse? Describe the incident and how you felt when you took even a little bit of control. Write a poem about it.

PART III

COURTSHIP AND
MARRIAGE, PRE-RECOVERY

Robyn Apffel

When I entered college, my parents moved across the country, so although I was only forty minutes from where I had grown up, I had the illusion of going away to college. My oldest sister had bought the family home from my parents, so it was still there, but it was her house now, and the most I would ever be was a visitor. That didn't seem like much of a change; I had always felt like a visitor anyway.

The day after my parents left, I was in the college library, staring out the window, feeling orphaned, when a young man came up from behind me and said, "Excuse me, but you don't look like you're getting very much done." "I'm not," I replied. "Well," he countered, "how would you like to go over to the snack bar with me for some coffee?"

That was how I met my husband Jim. I have never liked coffee, but I suffered through it because that was what had been offered, and assertiveness would not even be suggested to me until a good twenty years later. Jim and I dated regularly for about a year when I became very serious about the relationship, and he bolted. After six months of absence, he called and asked me to go out again. I agreed, but I was cautious throughout the evening because I wasn't really sure why he had called again. He had needed that time to figure out what he wanted from this relationship, and when he did, he reappeared into my life, ready to make a commitment to marriage if I were willing. I was.

I can't remember exactly what my expectations of marriage were back then. I know that I believed marriage was something to be created, as if it were an unnatural state that had to be designed and carefully worked out. I also know that my architectural plans for marriage were unrealistic and that they demanded the same sacrificial attitude of me that my relationship with my parents had demanded. I approached marriage with the firm belief that I had to make all the compromises and adjust to whatever Jim wanted. Let me be clear: Jim never asked or expected that of me, and probably was not even aware that I was doing it. Just as the word "assertiveness" was not then in vogue, neither was the word "co-dependency." I knew only one thing for sure when I entered into marriage: I was not going to be like my mother.

I hated the way my mother treated my father, and I have no doubt that her domineering nature contributed greatly to my father's molesting me in order to gain some sense of possessing masculine power. As an adult, I can understand the human frailties of both of my parents, even if I am unaware of the specific origins of those weaknesses, but as an eighteen-year-old in search of a husband, I had no such understanding. I knew only that I was not going to be like my mother, nor would I marry a man who was even remotely like my father. Having categorically dispensed with the two role models life had provided me, I needed to create my own definitions of "masculinity," "femininity," and "marriage."

My definitions were composites of myth, literature, 1960's vintage TV, and wishful thinking. Not only were my definitions fiction-based, but the way I went about living them was equally unreal. I lived life as if it were a script, and if something didn't quite work in rehearsal, then I would adjust the script and re-do the scene until I got it perfect. What I didn't realize until nearly twenty years into the marriage was that even if I did get it perfect, it was still nothing more than a script, fictional, unreal, as much a lie as the pretending I did as a child that I came from a "good" family.

While I had always believed that if we lived long enough we would have a twenty-eighth anniversary, or a fiftieth for that matter, I was not always very certain that we would celebrate it. Jim and I lived many years in the unhappy state of commitment to the marriage and to the children, but with an absence of desire for each other, and neither one of us with the guts to talk honestly to the other.

In my script of the perfect marriage, the man was strong, physically, emotionally, and psychologically. The man was the leader, the head of the household. The reality is that Jim is a good man, but he is not a leader. He has high moral standards; he is stable, reliable, a hard worker, honest, caring, pleasant, and devoted to his family. I have never for an instant questioned his fidelity, and I have always known that he loves me more than anything else on the face of this earth. But he's not perfect and if I had known earlier what I know now, I would not have expected him to be. I would have realized that he is human, imperfect by definition, and I can love him anyway, just as he loves imperfect me.

Before Jim and I were married, I told him what my father had done to me. He said it was okay, as if all I needed was to be reassured that he would accept me even though I was damaged goods. And we never spoke of it again . . . not until eighteen years later when I finally mustered the courage to face the truth about both my childhood and my marriage. Throughout all those years, the sexual abuse I had suffered as a child stood squarely between me and my husband. He never pressured me for sex because he thought he understood, without discussing it with me, how I felt about it. Jim is a truly nice man, probably the easiest man in the world to get along with, and he welcomed my physically abusive mother and my sexually abusive father into our home with the same warmth as he would welcome our best friends. It hurt me deeply, but I never told him so. My role, after all, was to be subservient, to allow him to be the head of the household, to make the major and minor decisions. In the early years of our marriage, even though I was working full-time as a teacher, contributing nearly as much to our finances as he was, everything I earned was deposited into his bank account, and I never spent a dime without consulting him. He never exactly denied me anything, but, then, it was totally outside of my script to even ask.

Jim has given me the space I need to grow, but he has not led me. He is genuinely satisfied with the status quo, and usually sees no need to change. I thrive on change, but for many, many years I allowed myself to stagnate rather than move ahead because I didn't want to threaten my husband's masculinity. Eventually, I came to realize that he is not threatened either by change nor my leadership. It is merely his nature to accept whatever is . . . if I stay the same, it's okay with him; if I change, that's okay, too. He never asked me to "stifle" myself. I made that choice entirely on my own because I needed not to be like my mother and I needed Jim not to be like my father. It took me far too many years to realize that there are countless patterns in between.

Over the years I have befriended several men who have filled my need to be challenged to grow spiritually, intellectually, and emotionally. At times, I have had to work through my emotional overdependence on these people and have had to get beyond a painful obsessiveness, but, in the end, these relationships have provided me with very, very, dear friends. Jim has accepted and encouraged these relationships because he has seen how alive and inspired I am when my needs for growth are being fulfilled. He also reaps great benefits from the changes in me and does not appear to feel threatened by my friendships. He did not have to trust them; he only needed to trust me, and he did. It may have been harder for me to get accustomed to having male friends than it was for Jim. I sometimes had to work to keep my feelings under control, but that can be done, particularly when everything is talked about openly. It has been wonderful for me to connect with men who are so different from my father: strong, moral, dedicated men who treat me as an equal, who lead and inspire me to be the best I can be, respecting my intelligence and considering me a friend. But I'm getting ahead of myself, as such relationships did not occur until much later, in my recovery period. In early marriage I would have looked only to my husband to supply all of my needs, regardless that no one person can do that for another.

The poems in this section are pre-recovery, and, again, contain insights that I surely did not possess at the time I was living the events depicted here. So thoroughly convinced was I that it was my duty to make all the compromises, that I was totally unaware how deeply I resented doing it. The resentment is evident in several of my poems, but it took me awhile to figure out where it was coming from; after all, I had made the choice to compromise. My choice, of course, had been based on a dysfunctional understanding of marriage, and I finally realized that my resentment stemmed from the fact that I was not present in this marriage. I began asking, "Is there any room in this relationship for me?" It was truly frightening to ask for more from my marriage, but when I did, Jim responded with a hearty, "Yes." He had never intended to deprive me, but he didn't know what I needed any more than I did, and, incidentally, he is every bit as co-dependent as I am. During his childhood, Jim's parents were very good to him, but they had also made their share of mistakes, so Jim entered our marriage with just as many insecurities as I had, only different ones. Neither one of us has ever been confrontational, and we had nary a clue how to face unpleasantness, so we usually avoided it. We both had much to learn, and it quickly became evident that we were not going to learn it from each other.

Between his inexperience and my history, really, what chance did we ever have of a normal sex life?

Intimacy was nearly non-existent in the early years of our marriage. We had conversation, but we did not know how to communicate; we had sex, but we did not know how to make love. As we began to talk honestly with each other, I shared my fears, my disappointments, and my opinions. We discovered that in spite of the many mistakes we had made in our marriage, we had survived them with strength and dignity. Jim told me that he had always hated my father for what he had done to me, and I asked him then how could he be nice to the man? He was merely treating my father as he treated his own, and thought that was what I had wanted. What I had wanted was for him to punch the man in the nose. It sometimes amazes me that we lasted nearly two decades like that, especially in this era of easy divorce, but neither of us considered divorce an option. In some of my fantasies when I envisioned myself being in a truly intimate marriage to someone else, my marriage to Jim simply didn't exist, but I never pictured divorce or abandonment. Jim and I both believe wholeheartedly in marriage, though I must hasten to add for the sake of the reader that I am talking about my marriage to this man. I do understand and agree with divorce when there is abuse, infidelity, or truly irreconcilable differences. Jim and I have never been unkind to each other, nor unfaithful, and our differences, once we began talking about them, were certainly reconcilable. We lived unnecessarily through too many unhappy years. Therapy would have benefitted us both, but I was the only one receiving it.

We do what we are ready for. We can't do otherwise. It was difficult for me to write the poems of the early years of marriage, to express disappointments in myself and in my husband. It felt like great disloyalty; after all, even my closest friends were stunned to find that my marriage was not as perfect quite as I had pretended it to be. At first, they reminded me what a wonderful man I was married to, and that angered me because it smacked of believing he was too good for me, but that was not what they had intended. I needed recognition that I was a valuable part of this marriage, too; I needed it from Jim, from our friends, from our family, and I needed to believe it too. I do now, and that belief is evident in the recovery chapter of this book. For this section, I will appear subservient, confused, hurt, and angry. I will seem to give my husband all the credit for being wonderful, but I will seem to resent him for it. Jim has read all these poems, and he agrees that they do represent the early years of our marriage. He agreed to have them included, and there were none that he declined. I thank him for that because I really needed the freedom to deal with this subject honestly in order to move ahead to where I became emotionally capable of writing the recovery poems that come later in this book.

PERSONAL AD

Single, scared female,
Who does a remarkable job
Of appearing confident and secure,
Seeks marriage-bound male
To share a life.

Applicant must be
Kind, patient, understanding,
Faithful and trustworthy;
Must be committed to
The institution of holy matrimony.

Will share financial burden
But is in desperate need
Of emotional security.
Will train;
No experience necessary.

WORTHY OF MY TRUST

Can I trust you?
Can I be sure that you won't hurt me?

Trust . . . that most fragile
Of all human emotions,
Built on the foundation of
Consistency, dependability, and love;
Evolving one kind action at a time
Unpunctuated by careless words;
Not always giving what is requested
But choosing every time what is right.

And it is so hard for me to trust!
Years of abuse, disappointment, betrayal
Have left me wary, cautious, shy,
Have sequestered me behind a forbidding wall
Holding the world at bay, watching with unquenchable
    suspicion,
Testing, setting elaborate traps,
Waiting for and expecting the fall.

Now you have successfully overcome my obstacles
And my mind accepts with full conviction
That you are, indeed, worthy of my trust.
My mind knows it, and knows it well,
But my emotions still churn in a sea of distrust.
My emotions refuse to succumb to logic,
Leaving me still questioning,
Can I trust you not to hurt me?

The question is no longer:
Are you worthy of my trust?
Rather: am I capable of trusting you
As much as you deserve?

IF THIS IS LOVE

If this is love,
Then I should be free
To be who I am,
To say what I believe,
To feel, unguarded.

If this is love,
Then I should tell you
About my fears and my failures,
Certain that you will not judge me,
Sure that you will forgive.

If this is love,
Then I should be real
And cast aside this mask
That hides and protects me
From the rest of the world.

If this is love,
Then I should feel secure
In your promises;
I should not fear
That you will abandon me.

How should I know
If this is love?
I must risk
Exposing my heart
And standing unshielded before you.

AS MUCH AS I CAN

You deserve better; I know it.
I love you as much as I possibly can,
Please be sure of that,
But I'm so afraid that it won't be enough,
That it won't match the love you give to me.

I accept your love gratefully
As if you offer it as a gift of charity,
And I, impoverished as I am,
Though I may give to you all that I own,
Will still remain deeply in your debt.

And I want to believe that love is not like that,
That love is not a ledger
In which credits must balance debits,
Nor a scorecard which records
The winner and the loser of the game.

I want to believe that if I give to you
As much love as I possibly can
In time my love may flourish and grow
To equal the love that you give to me.
Meanwhile, please be satisfied with all the love
   I have to give.

YOU NEED TO KNOW

I've never revealed this before to a soul,
I'm so ashamed,
But there's something you need to know,
And if you decide then that you don't want me,
I'll understand; I'll let you go.

I'm not a virgin; I'm not untouched;
I am not pure.
But there's something you need to know.
I have never given myself willingly
To any man; never have I ever made love.

My innocence was ripped away from me,
I'm so embarrassed,
But this is something you need to know:
I was raped and I was molested
A hundred times, no, even more.

I swear I neither asked for nor wanted it,
I was defenseless,
And there's something else you need to know.
I was but a child when it happened
And it was my father who despoiled me so.

Since then, no man has ever touched me,
I've been so guarded,
And this you need to know,
That freely I place myself in your hands,
I'm giving myself now to you.

As I offer with courage my body and soul,
I'm terrified,
But there's something you need to know:
I'll understand if you reject me;
It will break my heart, but I'll go.

ONE WOODEN HORSE ALONE

I was one wooden horse alone,
Unbending, unmoving but for the soft rocking motion
Caused by the wind.
I couldn't have moved even if I'd wanted to,
And I didn't want to,
For I had been out in the world
And had found it to be
Cold, scary, and dangerous.
Here I had found a home
That was warm, safe, and comfortable.

Here I stood, one wooden horse alone
Among the daisies and buttercups,
Amidst the lush green grass of summer.
Here I stood with golden rays of sunshine
Burnishing my chestnut coat.
Here I stood and scrutinized every detail of my
    surroundings
Until I was certain
That there was nothing here that could hurt me.

As I stood alone,
Unbending, unmoving but for the soft rocking motion
Caused by the wind,
Something caught my eye,
Something that moved,
Something that I had never seen before,
Something that did not belong in my private, secluded
 haven.
I didn't know whether I should run away
Or stay to defend my property,
But the choice wasn't mine to make,
For I was riveted to the spot where I stood,
Unable to move, frozen with fear.

And so I watched as you approached me.
As you came nearer I could see
That you were very much like me,
With the sun picking up the red highlights
Of your warm chestnut coat,
Your ebony mane blowing with the wind
As you cantered toward me.

There was something gentle in your confident manner,
Something that piqued my curiosity;
There was something inviting in your eyes
And something soothing in the soft tone of your voice
That secured my trust.
I spoke with you,
Hesitantly at first, because it had been so long
Since I had spoken to anyone,
But soon I could feel myself relax
And in a few short moments
You and I were laughing together,
Sharing our thoughts, our hopes, our dreams,
Talking of sharing our lives.

I asked you to stay here with me in my meadow home,
But you refused me,
For you said that you could not survive
In my sterile, protected, artificial environment.
You invited me instead
To go with you into the world
Where I would become alive like you,
To walk by your side, to live and to love.
You told me that you would help me find
Beauty and truth
In a world that I had presumed devoid of both.

Now the choice was mine to make
And I chose life with you.
Your touch released my pent-up energy
And the look in your eyes transfused me
With the courage I needed to loose my stiffened joints.
I strode with you across my familiar beloved meadow
And crossed into the unknown,
Unsure of what I would find there,
But utterly secure in your love and care.
Briefly I paused to look back as you moved on,
But I turned my head and in a few short steps
I was once more by your side,
Never again to stand
As one wooden horse alone.

Marriage Vows

White lace gowned and veiled in illusion
With familiar music pacing my trembling steps down
    the aisle,
Arm-in-arm with the man who had damaged me,
I approach the altar to present myself to you.

You stand stiffly looking as frightened as I feel
As you reach out to take my hand as your bride,
Accepting me with all my history and all my
    possibilities
An equal partner with whom you will share your life.

A stranger who seems to have known the requisites of
    marriage
Wrote our promises for us long ago,
Vows of intention that will undergird our union
And point the direction when we would otherwise
    lose our way.

The terms are unconditionally binding, always,
    forever,
With no "if clauses," no provision for escape,
Dependent upon will more than on passion,
Pre-demanding forgiveness of all future wrongs.

The full weight of God's commandment rests upon us
As we divest ourselves of our singleness
And leave it behind on the altar
To begin our sacred journey together till death us do
    part.

Robyn Apffel

A MAP FOR THE JOURNEY

Her youth was spent on the barren plains.
She had survived that inhospitable terrain
And had found the fresh promise
Of flowing waters and green fertility
In the eyes of her groom
Standing by her side
At the verge of the frontier,
A virgin territory unknown to any of her ancestors.

She had paid the exorbitant price of her passage
With her innocence and her tears
And carried in her baggage the family honor
And a map she had carefully drawn for the journey,
A product of her own imagination.
The Promised Land, she was determined,
Would bear absolutely no resemblance
To the desert she was leaving behind.

The map itself was truly a work of art
With black ink tracings on mottled buff parchment,
Shadings of pigment meticulously applied
Representing mild curves and gradual contours
Of a land rich and inviting
With rivers that are wide but easy to cross,
Hill slopes that are gentle, sunlit, carpeted,
Highways that are safe and convenient.

Endearing rustic communities dotting the map
Is each a haven of hospitality and acceptance
For the journey-weary traveler,
A home of harmony for its residents,
A place where children
Can run and play and grow in safety,
Where people are respected
Simply because they are people.

With her precious map in her hands,
She and her husband immigrated into this land
To begin their hope-filled new life together.
Her map guided their first new steps
Delivering them into a home of their own
Built on the foundation of love and trust.
But too soon they discovered that the map did not conform
To the real properties of the ground on which they stood.

The uncomfortable land was seductively familiar,
Not very different from the place of her birth,
For although it was not openly hostile, it was,
Nevertheless, lacking the nutrients she needed to grow.
Panicked, she attempted to force the land
To comply with her rendering,
Refusing to surrender her interpretation
Of how the earth ought to be.

She toiled at making the territory fit her map
As if by sheer will she could reshape the world,
Superimposing her own creation upon reality
Expecting that the beauty of what she desired
Would overcome the banality of what really was.
Her map became her useless companion, feeding her
    frustration,
Fueling her disillusionment, dragging her down,
Just like the baggage she had carried from her homeland.

A Stranger in Paris

My heart is a stranger here
In Paris, the city of love.
I wander from one grand site to another,
Giddy, my eyes and mouth open wide
Drinking in, tasting the awesome view,
Trying to make some sense
Of this unfamiliar territory.

Pedestrians dart with confidence past me;
This is the city of their birth
And they know where they are going.
They seem not to notice me,
A stranger helpless as a newborn,
Pleading for someone to guide me
Safely across the bustling boulevard.

But I don't speak their language
And they have no patience
To struggle to comprehend mine.
So I stumble and I stammer
Using awkward phrases, poorly chosen words,
Pronunciation so distantly amiss
That no one here can understand me.

I know nothing about Paris,
Her structures as noble as love itself,
Her streets a tangled web
Of veins, arteries, capillaries
That chokes my determined heart.
I must find my own way to demystify Paris
So I can make my home in this city of love.

SHARON'S SECRET

It stands shrouded by layers of time,
Pleats of the past tucked prudently in place
To hide her private embarrassment, shame,
Invisible now, no, transformed
Into an elaborate, shimmering lie
So real, so utterly credible
That Sharon herself can almost believe
That her pretense of innocence is true.

But love, love demands honesty
And commands her to share with David
The secret she has veiled from all others,
To bestow upon him as the centerpiece of her dowry
A gift more precious than jewels or gold,
More rare than virginal freshness,
Her sacrificial offering of truth
About her pain, her brokenness, her humanity.

And love demands that he accept it.
He holds her blameless as he hears her confession
And shoves it deep down into his pocket,
Stuffing it down with his disappointment,
Padding it with his fears and uncertainty,
Resolving to muffle its voice forever.
And so it is that Sharon's secret
Becomes David's secret as well.

It remains in the folds of the present
Closed to inspection or discussion;
Thickly spread with antiseptic ointment
That conceals, but offers no comfort;
Bandaged with a silence that will not bring healing;
Sutured with the offending infection yet inside,
Inside two of them now instead of just one,
Sharing a disease that consumes them both.

NOTHING OF SIGNIFICANCE

She wants to talk with him
About everything that has happened to her
That has left her frightened and confused.
    He is very uncomfortable;
    That topic is taboo.
She wants him to know
All about her insecurities
And to help her overcome them.
    He married her, didn't he?
    Nothing to talk about there.
She wants to share her dreams with him,
To tell him of the heights she hopes to climb,
To point to the stars she wishes to grasp.
    How unrealistic, foolish!
    No reason to even talk about it.
She wants him to teach her,
Guide her, challenge her to grow,
Encourage her to become the best she can be.
    He's satisfied with her just as she is.
    What's there to talk about?
She wants him to listen, just listen,
As she verbally explores new ideas
Of how to handle life's situations.
    He thinks she wants solutions.
    He doesn't give her the opportunity to
        talk.

She needs him to accept her tears
Of genuine pain and frustration,
Honest expression of her feminine emotions.
    He can't handle that at all.
    She swallows the tears.
She needs to talk with him
About all the things in life, past, present,
    future,
That truly matter to her, to him, to them.
    He is uneasy and would rather talk
    About nothing of significance.

CHAMELEON

I can change.
I am yours.
I do not possess myself.

I can be tropical vermilion
Sizzling fire
Fluid butterscotch lava
Gushing, flowing, trickling
Sticky sweet;
Shocking primaries,
Undiluted secondaries,
No white to soften,
No hint of gray to mute.

I can be temperate gold
Warm to touch
A paint store palette offering
Rainbow related shades:
Aquamarine, seafoam, moss,
Apricot, melon, dusty rose,
Cornsilk, jonquil, straw,
Peach, pumpkin, rust,
Amethyst, periwinkle, grape.

I can be polar frost
Cool reservation
A frozen pillar of isolation
Distant, distinct
Miles between your shadow and mine.
Stark white, solid black
Indefinable gray
Fleeing unattainable
Spilling into the night.

I do not inhabit myself.
I am yours.
I can change.

BARBIE AND KEN

Hard plastic
Exaggerated perfection
Arthritic joints
Unseeing
Unknowing
Unreal
> Unliving
> In a dreamhouse
> Sterile
> Pink
> Yellow, blue, white
> Paper decals
>> Their only statement
>> Fashion
>> Dictated by
>> Glossy magazines
>> Pop culture
>> Tradition
>>> Red convertible
>>> Swimming pool
>>> Trappings of success
>>> No family
>>> No problems
>>> No life

PATCHWORK

Ancestral hand-me-down bed covering
Patterned by the generations
Obediently hand-stitched
Quarter-inch flat seams
Precisely mitered corners
Measured right angles
Smooth and even joints
Traditional block-by-block repetition

Predictable
    Monotonous
        Confining
            Binding
            Rejected
        Abandoned
    Hated
Disposed

Crazy quilt cut with no pattern to guide
Design emerges spontaneous
Imitating nothing
Singular shapes of calico
Irregular bits of gingham
Blatantly mismatched colors
Loosely seamed unrefined
Unique combinations a variegated whole

Individual
Creative
Fluid
Modern
Untested
Unskilled
Made of scraps
Patchwork

THREE PACES

You never asked me to walk
Three paces behind you;
You asked me to walk by your side.
You never wanted to be
Both captain and navigator;
You preferred that we share sailing duties.
You never locked me inside
Close restricting walls;
You gave me all the space I needed to move.
You never posed limitations
Upon my associations or friendships;
You afforded me full freedom to choose.
You never silenced me
From expressing my opinions;
You always valued my counsel.
You never tried to impose your will on me
Or mold me into your image;
You accepted me as I am.

It was I who decided
That you should lead
And I should follow.
I wanted you to be the man
That my father never was
For my mother or for me.
I required you to be
Strong and decisive and firm
In your actions and in your words.
I wished that you would have told me
About life in the real world
About which I knew so little.
I longed to be held
Closely and tightly and securely
And never let go.
I needed you to guide me
Into maturity so I could become
The mate you needed me to be for you.

CHINA DOLL

Hold her gently, Dear.
Take care, for you might break her.
Remember, she's a china doll,
With cheeks blushed on like rose petals,
Lips applied in a wishful smile,
Blue eyes painted unchangeably in a hopeful stare.
Charming she is, perfect,
But very delicate, a china doll.
Dress her in lace and organdy
With flowers and ribbons
Upon her golden curls.
Set her carefully upon the chaise
In the drawing room of your dolls' house.
She is a lady,
Made for sitting and reading and needlepoint;
Soft-spoken, dreaming of love;
Made to be looked at; made to be protected;
Made to be treasured.
Handle her carefully; she is a china doll.

I won't break! Go ahead, touch me.
I won't break, you'll see.
God made me strong
To withstand the trials of living in this world.
He made me pliable and resilient
So the storms cannot snap me in two,
So that I will not shatter if you let me fall.
Look at me! You can see
That my face is not a frozen mask.
My wishful smile asking for your love
Can easily change to disappointment
Should you refuse me
Or to a satisfied grin
Should you fulfill my desires.
My eyes can sparkle like sunlight,
Study you intensely,
Fill with murky pools of tears, or even close into sleep.
I want to be dressed
So that I can move, walk, run, work.
Yes, I'm a lady,
A lady made for intimacy of thought, spirit, and feeling;
Made to be held, kissed, touched, loved;
Made to share with you the bad as well as the good.
God made me to live in this world,
To be a vital part of it, to feel its pains and pleasures;
To learn how to love in spite of life.
God made me real.
I am not a china doll.

ROSANNA

Silks and laces . . . crystal and china . . .
Music and poetry . . . laughter and smiles . . .
Softness and loving . . . giving, forgiving . . .
Radiance and goodness . . . Rosanna.

Harsh words . . . hard roads . . .
A world full of savages . . .
A perilous trip . . .
Gather your treasures and hide them, Rosanna.

Wrap them in cotton . . .
Protect them from danger . . .
Bury them deep . . .
Trust no one to see.

Denim and leather . . . tin and wooden . . .
Shouting and silence . . . heartaches and tears . . .
Cold and unmoving . . . unwilling to blossom . . .
With lackluster surface denying your wares.

A gentle man finds you . . .
Sees through your defenses . . .
He's guessed at your secret . . .
He gives you his love.
He holds and protects you . . .
Resets your journey . . .
Toward comfort, security,
Clear skies, smooth roads.

A home in the forest . . .
The laughter of children . . .
Years of commitment . . .
Voices of friends.

Rosanna, Rosanna,
Rediscover your treasures . . .
Open your baggage
And let love shine in.

Silks and laces . . . denim and leather . . .
Crystal and china . . . wooden and tin . . .
Music and poetry . . . shouting and silence . . .
Smiles and laughter . . . heartache and tears.

Growing and giving . . . now willing to blossom . . .
Exposed to the danger . . . exposed to the light . . .
Singing of freedom . . . sharing your treasures . . .
Open to love now . . . now open to life.

TEARS ALONE

I share my smiles with strangers I pass casually on the
    streets;
I share my laughter with family and friends;
I share my knowledge with my students
And my thoughts with my colleagues;
I share my talents with those who appreciate them;
I share my hospitality with my guests;
I share my wealth with people all across the world
Whom I may never meet and never know their names;
I share my home with my husband and children;
I share my dreams with those I love;
I share my time with many;
I share my gifts with any who have need of them;
I share my body with only my husband;
But I shed my tears alone.

MECHANICAL ADVANTAGE

Well, the mechanical advantage
Is most definitely yours:
My power of resistance is much lesser
Than your potential strength of force.

But you willingly regulate
The capacity of your engine;
So I correspondingly agree
To allow a coupling with you.

It is purely mechanical, after all:
Two complex machines
Engaging their complementary parts
In rhythmic mutual motion.

There's nothing personal about it;
Merely an application
Of immutable laws of physics:
    Energy, motion, resistance, force.

A Different Touch

His touch was invasive.
It barged through my gates
Without even asking
For permission to enter.
It grabbed me unaware
And wrestled me roughly
To the dirty floor.
It was coercive and enslaving
And totally humiliating.
His touch was repulsive.

Your touch is respectful.
It reaches out its hand
Extending it for me to hold.
It approaches me face-to-face
And grants me the freedom
To stay or to run away. It awaits my response.
It offers me comfort
And safety and shelter.
Your touch is inviting.

If I resist your touch
Do not be offended.
I am not threatened by you
But by the residue of his violation
That is stuck like slime inside me.
Although your touch has the power
To heal my wounded emotions
It will take time and much patience
For me to learn
How to feel touch without pain.

A Spectator Sport

You and I are here alone
On the playing field,
Not a fan in the grandstand,
No vendors hawking hot dogs or soda,
No cameramen or reporters,
No coaches, managers,
No other teammates,
Just you and I.

I'm not really sure
What game we're playing here.
There is no arrangement
Of goals or bases,
No yard lines
Or divisions of a court.
There is simply a playing field,
Unmarked, rectangular, and flat.

You and I have not discussed
The rules of the game;
You just expect me to know them.
I did play something like this
When I was a kid,
But not quite the same
Because now the man I'm playing with
Is not my opponent.

I didn't like the game
Very much back then.
The man who taught me to play
Liked it a lot
And he always wanted
To engage in the sport,
But I didn't think it was much fun.
I tried quitting the team;
I didn't show up for practices;
I avoided the field altogether.

But I like being here with you now.
It's a brand new stadium,
One that you and I
Planned and built together.
The season is right
And I have agreed to play on your team.
I'm certain that I can win this game
If only I play it with you.

The first quarter of the game
Is really quite fun
And we move well together.
But soon, you start running
Way too fast for me to keep up,
And that confuses me
So I ask you to tell me
What I'm supposed to do.

You tell me not to worry,
That I don't need to do anything,
Just lie there, and let you score the points.
Suddenly this game is very familiar,
Just the way I remember it
From when I was a kid.
I still don't like it very much,
But at least now I know what to do.

I take off my uniform
And lie flat on my back,
Motionless in the middle of the field
Until you triumphantly cross the goal line.
And me? I feel like a piece of equipment,
Not a valued teammate,
Not even a participant,
A spectator of an impersonal sport.

A TASTE OF HONEY

He was raised on a nutritious diet
Consisting of meat, dairy, whole grain,
Lots of vegetables, and occasionally,
Fresh fruits as a special treat.

Mealtimes were punctual and orderly;
Servings were measured with care;
He sat at the table until his plate was clean;
Over-indulgence was strictly forbidden.

He's never tasted honey, so he has no way of knowing
How enticingly sweet it can be.
He has learned to be completely satisfied
With just a sprinkling of sugar and spice.

He walks past the finest confectioneries,
Passes by Viennese pastry shops,
Goes right on by ice cream parlors
With no consideration of taking a taste.

He goes home now to his wife's kitchen
And shares with her a plain-cooked meal,
No fancy stuff and certainly no dessert,
But he is satisfied all the same.

COMPLAINT DEPARTMENT

May I help you, Ma'am?
> *I hope so. I need to change my husband.*

I see. Whom would you like to exchange him for?
> *No, no! I want to keep him. I just want to change him, that's all.*

How long have you had him, Ma'am?
> *Ten years.*

That's a long time, Ma'am. When did you notice that he's defective?
> *He's not defective!*

Then why do you want to change him?
> *Because I've changed.*

I see. What exactly do you want to change about him?
> *I'd like him to be more interested in sex.*

Has his interest in sex decreased since you got him?
> *No, it's pretty much the same. That's what attracted me to him in the first place. I felt safe with him.*

And you don't feel safe with him now?
> *Oh, I feel safe all right! Too safe! But I'm ready to live a little more dangerously now.*

Let me see if I understand: You married him because he wasn't interested in sex, and now you want to change him to make him more interested in sex. Is that right, Ma'am?
> *Yes, that's right.*

I'm sorry, Ma'am. I don't think we can do that. May I direct you to our cosmetics department? Lingerie?

OLD FLANNEL PAJAMAS

She's first to be ready for bed
So while he showers
She turns down the covers,
Sprinkles the sheet
With rose-fragranced powder,
Lights two slender candles
And turns off the lamp.
She fluffs their plump pillows
And sets them close together
At the top of their king sized bed.

She slips into her new nightgown,
Its narrow lace straps
Arching across her shoulders
From back to breast,
Satiny nylon sweetheart plunge
Revealing the fullness of her curves,
Across her hips, over her thighs,
Below her knees to her ankles.
There she lies on her side
And smiles when he enters the bedroom.

He is wearing his old flannel pajamas
And to his perception
She wears exactly the same.
He sees familiar, boxy, plaid,
Buttoned securely throat to navel,
Bottoms drawn tight at the waist,
Just like she's always worn,
Just the way he loves her.
He blows out the candles,
Climbs into bed, and goes to sleep.

PAS DE DEUX

We will dance the ballet some other time,
Some other time we will dance the grand pas de deux,
You the premier danceur and I prima ballerina,
We will perform some night together onstage.

Your entrance will be choreographed energy,
Confident motion, leaping with strength,
Stretching each muscle fiber to its fullest length,
Extending your irresistible invitation for me to join.

And I will! With nimble chassé excitement
I will take my place whisper-close at your side,
My stance arabesque, my arms allongé,
Your stance demi-pointe, your hands burning soft at my
    waist.

I will dance the adagio, slow, graceful, sustained;
I will rise as an angel in flight
My wings full and free reaching toward heaven,
My body supported en l'aire by the strength of your hands.

You will dance your pas seul with allegro
And pleasure me with your great finesse,
Rapid succession of acrobatic movement,
Cabriole, ballonée, ciseaux, jeté.

And then I shall dance for you, perfect simplicity,
Plié, brisé, piqué, relevé, gliding into pirouettes,
Exploding into a dizzying series of fouettés,
Slowing, slowing, bending willowy toward you in
 épaulement.

Our coda will be exquisite, grand finale,
Your body and mine performing as one.
We will stand face-to-face, our lips barely touching,
Our arms wrapped loosely in simulated embrace.

Your hands will skim my limbs, shoulders to fingertips,
Then you will lift me high above the stage,
My spine deeply arched as a swan in a dive,
I will fly in great circles as you spin below.

You will set me down gently, I landing light on my toes,
And we shall spin together, ever faster, ever faster,
Wild excitement, straining, straining every muscle,
Tense, tense, so deliciously satiated with tension.

We will embrace the moon; we will kiss the stars!
We will descend, softly as a feather in a windless sky,
Unwinding, disengaging, remaining whisper-close,
Bowing to each other the deep bow of professional respect.

And we will remain onstage until dawn
Breathing the incomparable sweetness of a fine
   performance,
You the premier danceur and I prima ballerina,
Our relentless commitment finding at last its great reward.

Some other time we shall dance that ballet;
We shall dance together that grand pas de deux;
You and I shall perform in the spotlight
Some other time . . . but not tonight.

Writing Prompts for Part III: Courtship and Marriage, Pre-Recovery

1. Re-read "As Much as I Can." How has the abuse undermined your self-esteem? Do you feel worthy of your own relationships? What value do you place on the love you give to others? Why should gratitude not enter into the equation of a mutually satisfying relationship? How does abuse corrupt the meaning of love? Write about that.
2. Re-read "A Map for the Journey." In what ways does your map almost guarantee that you will get lost in your marital journey? Do you insist on using your map to travel by, or are you willing to use the map of your spouse? Is your spouse's map any better than yours? Write a poem describing the accuracy or inaccuracy of your map.
3. Re-read "China Doll." Does your spouse treat you as if you might break? Do the people around you right now, people you love and who love you, walk on eggshells around you, afraid to tell you the truth, afraid to say or do anything that might upset you? How is your spouse overprotective of you in an effort to make up for the abuse you suffered at someone else's hands? Write about your strengths.
4. Re-read "Rosanna." Pay attention to the extremes and notice how the poem ties the two extremes together. In what ways has being abused led you to see things in a black or white contrast? Explore the grays in between. Write your own poem.
5. Re-read "A Spectator Sport." Write a poem comparing sex with your spouse to the act of

sexual abuse. How are they similar? How are they different? How has the abuse colored your attitudes toward sex? Write a poem exploring the parallels between your two separate experiences.

6. Re-read "Complaint Department." Think of what attracted you to your spouse. Were any of the attributes you most desired then based on your need to be protected? Was your spouse very eager to protect you? As you have grown, how has any of that changed? Did you both change together, or has one of you been left behind? Explore how your relationship with your spouse has changed since you first decided to marry, and write about that.

PART IV

BODY ISSUES, MY PHYSICAL REALITIES

When I began writing this book, I dove into "The Early Years" section with optimism and enthusiasm; likewise, "Twelve to Twenty," "Courtship and Marriage," and "Recovery." On "Body Issues," I shrank, wrestled, and procrastinated, and even considered dispensing with this section altogether . . . the book was already long enough . . . I ought to save something for my next book . . . this issue is too personal and my experiences are not universal enough for me to offer any expertise. The truth of the matter is that many of my body issues remain very much unresolved, and if I write about them, I just may have to do something about them, and that is not a task I am eager to undertake. It is gratifying to be able to write poems from an "I'm finished with this" perspective, to point to my own personal victories and to be proud of how far I've come. It is perhaps more essential, however, to be willing to put my vulnerabilities on the line and confess that I am nowhere near finished. Thus it is that the "Body Issues" poems are my work-in-progress, a rough sculpture in need of much refinement, a sketch that only hints at the finished product.

For me the greatest body issue has been acknowledging that I have one. It has been so easy for me to live in my mind and consider only my soul, ignoring the body's existence altogether. The body has been an inconvenience, something that requires more care than I wish to expend for even minimal maintenance, and, believe me, that is all I have given it. I have been fortunate to have rather good health, so I have not had to be aware of my physical needs. As I write this, my teeth are hurting. I'm nearly fifty years old, and three months ago one of my teeth cracked and broke off around its amalgam filling, but it didn't start hurting until last week, so I saw no need to take care of it. I have always been overweight, more seriously since bearing children, my youngest now fifteen years old, but even though I am intelligent enough to understand the finest points of nutritional study, I have never accepted emotionally that weight and food consumption are even remotely connected. From time to time I have made attempts at dieting and exercising, usually to please someone else or from some intellectual commitment to self-improvement. Whenever my life has demanded prioritizing my time, I have opted to read, write, or create rather than move.

Friends and therapists have suggested that my disinterest in the care of my body is due to low self-esteem and that if I thought more highly of myself I would be more concerned about my health and longevity. I have always resisted that explanation because I have believed that I do value myself highly. The choices I have made in every other area of my life confirm my self-esteem. I have concluded that I simply have not viewed my body as part of me. I define myself in terms of my mind and spirit, and if you were to ask me to tell you what I am like, the last thing I would think to mention would be my physical characteristics. I am what I think, what I believe, and what I do; I am what I create; I am my words.

More than anything else but love, words have the power to motivate me. On a bulletin board near the gym at the school where I teach is a highly understated poster which states simply, "If you don't take care of your body, where will you live?" While appeals to my vanity and to my intellectual understanding of health issues may fall on deaf ears, that simple question posted on the bulletin board prompts action for me. I believe absolutely in the eternal soul, so I have no difficulty dealing with passage from this earth, but I also believe that there are certain things that I must accomplish during this lifetime. My children are rapidly approaching adulthood, but they have not yet arrived; they still need a mother. My husband is anticipating retirement and would like someone to share it with. I have acquired much wisdom from the years, personally and professionally, and it would be a waste not to share it with several classrooms full of young people who are open to receiving it. I have come to believe that this book is an obligation in my life. My memories and my thoughts are in my brain, nowhere else. If I don't write this book, it will never be written, and I need my whole body to write the words that express the poetry of my soul.

I have experienced the world through the senses of my body and I have treasured relationships and the infinite beauty of this world. And yet I have denied the very body that affords me the opportunities to know the people I love so dearly as well as the earthly delights. Do I deny my body because of the sexual and physical abuse it received when I was just a child, just beginning to figure out where I fit into this world? Most certainly so! I clearly remember overhearing my parents discussing the fact that I would not cry during beatings of punishment. My mother was concerned that she would not know when to stop; my brother and sisters, at least, would cry and scream so she would know when they had had enough; but I remained stoically silent, so she couldn't tell. Of course it was intentional on my part. My body had been the receptor of far too much pain in my early years, so I simply shut it down and refused to feel whatever pain was inflicted upon me. The easiest and most effective way to do that was to dissociate, to detach from my body completely; it's not so hard to do. The parts of myself that I have valued highly, my mind and my spirit, could not be touched.

My body, on the other hand, suffered because of the physical abuse at the hands of my mother and the sexual abuse doled out by my father, whether I dissociated or not. The effects of their abusiveness on my body were temporary; the effects of my own neglect of my body have been long-range. Can I learn as an adult to dispense with my dysfunctional opinions of the body human? Again, most certainly so. It has taken me half a century, however, just to realize that my opinions have been dysfunctional. As long as my definition of myself included nothing regarding the body, there was no need to tend to it; but that is beginning to change. My soul may be eternal and my relationship with God may not be dependent on my physical being, but everything I do here on earth does require my physical presence, and I have many people here to love, much to give, much left to learn, and much to teach.

So it is time to consider my physical being, in poetry because that is where what I know and what I need to learn all come together. As I began writing the poems in this chapter, I quickly realized that the tone of these poems was quite different from that of the other poems I had already written. They were lighter, almost whimsical, and revealed to me that, while I take my mind and spirit very seriously, I do regard my physical being with less sense of urgency and much more humor. I also realized that the sarcastic nature of the humor I employed belied my claim to not taking the brevity of life very seriously. I want this life to be as long as possible, and I want this life to overflow with meaning. I want my life to increase the measure of the lives of others by leaving something valuable behind, something that only I can leave. I'm not concerned about having my name or face be remembered beyond my family and circle of friends, but I would like to have my words be remembered for having touched the common chords that have meaning to every one of every time and place.

I make my commitments in words before I make them in action, so perhaps the words of my own poems will guide me through the maze of understanding the workings of my own body and lead me toward better health and the longevity I will need to accomplish on this earth what is required of me, and in the process I may just learn to enjoy it.

MORE THAN THAT

Yes, I am mind and emotion
I am what I think and what I feel
I am the sum of my beliefs and devotions
But I am more than that
I am my body too
Skin and muscle blood and bone
I am nerves and organs
Involuntary bodily processes
In which I grow and age
In which I will die and decay

I accept that my body is real
It will feel pleasure and pain
It will know health and infirmity
It will place its trust in me
To care for it
To nurture it wisely
To exercise it regularly
To rest it when it tires
My body is part of my being
More than just a home for my mind and soul

HOUSEKEEPING

I did not know I'd stay so long
it is all only temporary you know
this life force trapped in organic bodies
subject to age and decay

dust accumulates on the sill
the dog tracks mud down the hallway
a cracked pane yields to the draft
the shingles leak and beams sag

I expected to be gone yesterday
so I neglected my housekeeping
considered it not worth the investment
of time or energy or resources

but my mind is growing and my spirit
demands more hours on this earth
for I have so much left to say
I must remain in this house awhile longer

it need not last forever
only enough days for me to complete
all the tasks destined for me
however long that may be

I will wipe the dust from the sill
scrub footprints from the floorboards
I will replace the window glass
patch the roof and shore up the beams

TAKE GOOD CARE OF YOURSELF

So you have been abandoned, neglected, abused:
You're a big girl now;
It's time you started taking care of yourself.
You may have been handed
A bodyful of bad habits:
You don't eat right;
You don't move enough;
You don't take the time to look your best;
But you're an intelligent woman;
There's nothing you can't learn to do.

So your parents didn't know how to love you:
It doesn't mean that you can't love yourself.
You know you're a valuable person;
You believe everyone is.
You have worked hard to do things right
And you have had many successes.
Forgive yourself your failures
And move forward toward your goals.
Take good care of yourself;
You deserve a huge slice of happiness.

EMBODIED

i have worn my silks
not so much to cover me
as to provide a dwelling place
for this disembodied soul

i have stuffed velvet sacks
with spiritual energy
and have required them to be
the visible expression of my life

my timid eyes have shown me
but the fabric of my femininity
flowing graceful in folds
from the top of my mind to the floor

my courage grown of late
i cast off my fear and with it
the gown that has concealed
the womanhood i have denied

garmentless now i view myself
embodied with torso and limbs
with flesh of breasts and belly
with face and features

i am finally aware
of the force of gravity
upon my skeleton and tissues
and of the weight I have carried

the great burden
i have shouldered so long
is not only the sackcloth of my past
but the very fiber of my body

FLIGHT OR FIGHT

someone else might run
from perceived danger
someone lean and muscular
might take flight
when faced with conflict
discomfort or uncertainty

that's not my style
i bulk up and hunker down
and prepare to fight
i don't run from nobody!
even when it might be safer
to flee than to stand my ground

i don't move so fast
and am paralyzed by fear
i do better to rely on my wit
and on my persistence
than on my speed
for long-term survival

the question is this:
has my endomorphic body
determined my fight personality
or has my propensity to fight
created my portliness?
and, can i change if i want to?

LEARNING TO BREATHE

breathe, robyn, breathe!
i remind myself
for sometimes i quite forget
that i need to exhale

life's gentle rhythms
strange to my body
casual breathing in and out
cleansing refreshing revitalizing

while i have known
gulp and gasp and hold
and hold and hold
turning vapor into carbon

robyn, breathe the airs of life
both fresh and foul
retaining the oxygen
and breathing out the waste

THEY SAY

They say
That sexually abused women
Overeat
So they will get so fat
That men find them unattractive
And will leave them
Alone.
I thought
I just liked chocolate.

They say
That sexually abused women
Overeat
To stuff down the pain
And to fill
The emotional void
Caused by the betrayal
Of their trust
By their fathers.
I thought
I just liked apple pie.

They say
That sexually abused women
Overeat
Because they learned
From their abusers
To expect
Instant gratification
And they cannot
Deny themselves pleasure.
I thought
I just liked candy.

They say
That sexually abused women
Overeat
Because they have
Low self-esteem
And they want to prove
That no one can love them
So they try
To kill themselves.
I thought
I just liked strawberry shortcake.

They say
That sexually abused women
Overeat
As a substitute
For being loved
Because they mistake
Quantities of food
For bona fide
Emotional nourishment.
I thought
I just liked chocolate chip cookies.

They say
That sexually abused women
Overeat
To use food like a drug
Like an addict
Because they will need
More ever more
To satisfy
Their emptiness.
I thought
I just liked hot fudge sundaes.

Satisfaction

Lying seductively on a crystal bed
Two soft creamy mounds melting
Dripping with warm sweet confection
Flowing like lava
Gathering in dark satin pools
Capped with snow white froth
Airy light lacy frill
Crowned with a glistening
Long-stemmed maraschino
I bring delicious to my lips
With a sterling silver spoon

THE HUMAN MACHINE

I dig my toes into the sand
Observing how my digital muscles
Move the hinges at the knuckles
And I know this is a voluntary motion
Willed by my brain
Its message transported from head to toe
And I am fully aware of the wonder
Of this machine that is my body

I studied the workings of the human body
In science class and health class
And I learned all about its systems
And how to keep it healthy
I understood it all
And got A's on my tests and report cards
But it was only head knowledge
And I never applied any of it to real life

Nutrition is not so difficult to understand
Nothing more than sums and ratios
Keeping track of what the body needs
Balancing vitamins and minerals and fiber
With the ubiquitous calorie
Extracting the greatest energy value
From the lowest caloric intake
And we all know what foods are healthy

But that's on paper and not on the plate
Sometimes I truly do believe that
My taste buds have a mind all their own
And that a pound of lettuce is the same
As a pound of chocolate nut fudge
A pound is a pound after all
So why should my body care
Whether I eat vegetable or butterfat

My intellectual brain surely knows
What is so and what is not
But my tongue chooses not to believe it
My stubborn self-indulgent tongue
Preferring the sweet
Of sugar and butter and chocolate
That contribute little to my health
But so much to my bulk

LIES I TELL MYSELF

I'll diet after Christmas
I'll begin an exercise program tomorrow
I'm already on a 1200 calorie diet
I'll give up chocolate for Lent
Some day I'll be a vegetarian

I have a large frame and heavy bones
All the women in my family are big
I can't lose weight
I don't want to lose weight
I don't care

Calories don't matter
Exercise doesn't matter
Diets don't work so why bother
If I lose weight I'll just gain it back
It doesn't matter what I eat

I can be healthy even if I am overweight
I can be happy even if I'm overweight
I can be self-confident even if I'm overweight
I do not define myself by my weight
I'm not embarrassed by my appearance

OLD HABITS

unpacking my groceries
after a hurried trip to the supermarket
i see the incontrovertible proof
of the power of my old habits

i must have skipped right by
the fresh produce aisle
for there is not a leafy green
nor a citrus fruit in my sack

there is a pound of gourmet bacon
a package of beef hot dogs
a tub of dutch potato salad
and deli-made turkey hoagies

in a separate plastic bag
i find white bread and rye
cinnamon toasting bread
and buns for the hot dogs

i chose the regular mayo
instead of the low-fat variety
and i never even read the labels
of the pre-packaged meals

i bought several bottles of fruit juice
blends actually that taste great
high in sugar content
but low in real fruit juice

i must have had a craving for chocolate
while i was at the store
for i am surprised to find
four six-packs of full-size bars

and i guess cola was on a great sale
because i purchased six two-liter bottles
and this was just a mid-week excursion
and of course with the pop we must have chips

a couple boxes of cereal
of the pre-sweetened kind
national brand cookies for the kids
and european style cookies for me

i've got all the fixings
for an italian dinner one night
a barbecue for the next
and a thanksgiving feast in july

it appears that i plan to do
a lot of home baking
but if i don't get around to it
i've a fine selection from the bakery

the two gallons of milk
ought to last us two days
and the cheddar and mozzarella and monterey jack
will make palatable many vegetable dishes
(if i had any vegetables)

eggs and butter and sour cream
seem to find their way
all by themselves into every order
that ends up in my home

there are boxes and cans
and frozen blocks
of prepared foods
that make my life just a little easier

i don't check the ingredients
for sodium or fat or cholesterol
and i don't concern myself
with balancing the food pyramid

i buy the familiar
the things that taste good
and satisfy my hunger
for delicious if not nutritious food

GOING TO THE HAIRDRESSER, AND OTHER ACTS OF COURAGE

My hair is too long and straggly
And the ends are split.
I shampoo, condition, curl, brush, arrange . . .
I do the best I can with it,
But I really do need to have it cut.
Beauty Salons . . . twelve yellow pages full . . .
Which one will I call this time?
I can't remember who I went to last;
It's been more than a year-and-a-half.
Perhaps if I went more often
I could establish a trust
And then it wouldn't panic me so much
To tilt my head back over the sink,
To sit, stiff, defenseless, chest upward,
While a stranger touches my hair and scalp
With lathered fingers.

This week, hairdressers;
Next week, doctors and nurses;
The week after that, mammogram X-ray technicians;
And then the dreaded dental hygienist
Followed by the dentist himself.
Thank God I don't have to go to a masseur,
A manicurist, or a proctologist!
I'm grateful for self-service shoe stores
And clothing bought off the rack.
Service with a smile,
A handshake, a pat on the shoulder,
An impersonal embrace.
Don't they all know how very painful it is
For me to let them touch me?

GETTING NAKED

Is it ever hard
to change my clothes
without getting naked
I pull my arms
in through the sleeves
and pull a clean shirt
over my head
and down
through the neck
of the dirty one
before I take that one off
I can't do that
with the pants
but at least
I can sit on the bed
doubled over
to hide my nakedness
until the clean ones
are safely over my hips

It's even harder
to take a bath
without getting naked
I wrap myself
in a big towel
and then remove
my clothing
and my underwear
and slide beneath the bubbles
strategically placing washcloths
to cover the pink of my skin
and then
when the water is cold
I pull the plug
and do the dance again
only this time
I do it in reverse

PERFUMES AND POWDERS

jasmine
full-bodied and feminine
moist
musky
delicate
sensuous and appealing
attracting
male sensibilities

finely milled talc
fragrant velvet
soothing
smooth
silky
dry lubricant
affordable luxury
too bad i'm allergic

GROOMING

time and attention
even pain
the inconvenience
of grooming

soap and water
not so bad
nor shampooing
and styling

manicure
pedicure
what a real cramp
in the hand and foot

but the absolute worst
the mammoth task
the drudgery
of hair removal

under the arms
the entire leg
above the lip
the brow

razor burn
tweezer ouch
wax and depilatory
nicks and rash

and it returns
and i remove it
and it returns
day after day

REACH OUT AND PUSH AWAY

With my right hand I reach out,
Palm receiving, open, upward,
Inviting your touch and accepting it.
With my left hand I push firmly away,
Palm vertical, strained slightly convex,
Refusing to clasp your comforting hold.

My trusting eyes welcome you
Into the privacy of my heart
And offer you residence there . . .
Only to block you at the final instant
With my trembling eyes that drive you away
From deeply hidden wounds.

With tender words I attempt to connect
With the part of you
That can understand and embrace me.
With brusque words I sever the tie
That threatens my peace of mind
And endangers my solitude.

I reach out to you
And I push away.

HUGS AND KISSES

I need to be hugged
As surely as I need to breathe.
I need a warm, human touch
To help my body forget
The insults and violation it has known.
I need to be held closely,
Tightly, lovingly,
In the safety of friendship
That asks no more than I can give.

I need to be kissed
Innocently, lightly, gently,
On the cheek or on the forehead
Or on my hand.
I need to feel valued and cared for
And protected from harm.
I need to believe in friendship
That will neither use nor abuse me,
That is concerned only for my benefit.

I trust my judgment;
I have grown and learned much,
And I know that good people
Are capable of loving-kindness,
That good people can help erase my pain.
I need hugs and kisses
From dear and wonderful friends.
I need to give my hugs and kisses
In return.

AN EXERCISE IN YOGA

It was offered as a gift
And I loved the giver
And trusted him
And wanted to receive
This exercise in yoga
In the spirit in which it was given

The music was calm and soothing
I was in the camaraderie of friends
In a place I thought of as home
It was a cool autumn evening
At the end
Of a fulfilling and exciting day

The room was filled
With the strong scent of acceptance
And I was part of it all
Knowingly and willingly
One member
In a community of twenty

I sat cross-legged on the floor
Just like all the others
And followed
The initial instructions
To breathe deeply in
Slowly and completely out

But unlike the others
I would not
I could not
Close my eyes
I could not release myself
To this naked vulnerability

And unlike the others
Who complied
With every instruction
Intended to relax
Both the body and the spirit
I resisted

My muscles tensed
My breathing became desperate
My mind shut down
And my emotions choked
As tears washed away
Any trust I'd had for this company

I stood up
And as quietly as I could
I left the room
And slunk into the dark hallway
Where I cried
And tried to regain my composure

My emotions
By refusing to allow
My body to submit
To someone else's control
Had robbed me of a gift
From a beloved and trusted friend

Robyn Apffel

A FRIENDLY TOUCH

it offers Comfort
and Waits for me to take Hold
Inviting me to Respond
but not insisting
it is non-invasive
Respecting
taking the time
making the effort to determine
my Boundaries
it is firm enough
for me to Trust
in its Sincerity
and for me to Know
that it is Real
with no painful pressure
not brute force
it stirs my blood
to feel Love
without lust
it Holds me so Close
that I feel Safe
but not aroused
it is the Touch
of Friendship

WONDERLAND

If I had visited Wonderland
When I was ten or eleven or twelve
Everyone would have smiled indulgently
And welcomed my naïve questions

But I'm forty
And for me to exhibit curiosity
About male and female anatomy
Is interpreted as perversion

There is so much I never learned
For I never asked
And never looked
And never listened

Way too early the world of sex
Was thrust upon me
So that I closed my eyes
My ears and my mind

Now faced with natural desires
I feel intimidated
By my own immaturity
Embarrassed by my ignorance

I want to feel sexual pleasure
And appreciate sexual beauty
I want to know sexual fulfillment
And believe that it is right and good

Silhouette

I have experienced my femininity
as if I were a silhouette
a two-dimensional shadow
an image with no substance

the mysteries of my womanhood
have been hidden even from me
as I have not dared to peer
beneath the undeniable surface

my female form merely suggests
the potential that lies within
to grasp a deep yearning for connection
to express my love by sexual union

with time a silhouette fades
and though it may be lovely
drawing its observer into its obscurity
it is but a fleeting presence in this world

MASCULINITY

take away
    all the personality requirements
    of the ideal husband
        the devotion
            generosity
            kindness
            honesty
take away
    his ambition
        stability
        intelligence
        persistence
            not that they're unimportant
            they are consummately so
            and one would be crazy to consider
            marrying
            without examining a man's attributes
but take them away
and consider for a moment
only a man's sexuality
    his passion
        eroticism
        libido
        appetite

consider
    his kiss
        touch
        attentiveness
        embrace
consider
    his potency
        strength
        endurance
        ability to sustain
consider
    his constancy of desire
        willingness to give
            and receive
                pleasure
                to be intimate
                and to be completely satisfied

WITHOUT INHIBITIONS

this is my husband
my intimate bed partner
the man I chose
to share my life
the father of my children

he has seen me
stripped of all pretense
in my messy humanity
weak, frail, uncertain
afraid of reality

he has witnessed
both my successes
and my failures
my glory
as well as my shame

he has touched
my flabby sagging
aging and wrinkling
not always fragrant
imperfect body

and he has loved me
and accepted me
as i lie next to him
vulnerable and exposed
without inhibitions

IT'S MY PLEASURE

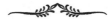

my pleasure is an embrace
full and close, one-to-one
holding firm and long
the man i love
who gives his love to me

it's my pleasure to kiss
warm and moist, lips-to-lips
tasting his tongue
exploring inside his mouth
and giving him the same of me

my pleasure is to touch
soft but convincing, skin-to-skin
for him to caress
my femininity and for me
to appreciate his virility

my pleasure is to be aroused
feverishly rushing, pulse-to-pulse
aching to be one
my blood racing through my veins
his engorging him to readiness

it's my pleasure to be satisfied
reaching our climax, body-to-body
bursting and breathless
releasing all our energy
into each other's arms

SOMEONE'S FANTASY

That I should be his fantasy
That he should wrap his arms
Around reveries of me
When he needs to be loved perfectly
And understood more deeply even
Than he can understand himself
Accepted for all of his complexities
The strengths he boldly exhibits
The weaknesses he endeavors to conceal
His lofty magnificent dreams
And his fears that he won't achieve them

That he should feel secure
In my ever constant love
More tolerant than his own
More forgiving of his shortcomings
More patient than his restless spirit can bear
To anchor him in my loving care
In someone he can trust
To be always firmly on his side
Who will hear him when he whispers
And affirm the beauty of his soul
The goodness of his heart

That he should be free
To create a glorious love story
Torrid passionate enduring comforting
Intimate to the very core
The penetrable center of his defenselessness
Where he can embrace me fully
And yet remain safely insulated
Untouched by an intrusive other
Uncompromised in his self-protection
Where the reality of my needs
Should impose no demands upon his fantasies

Writing Prompts for Part IV: Body Issues, My Physical Realities

1. Re-read "Housekeeping." How has life surprised you? Are you more hopeful about living a long, successful life than you once were? How does this hopefulness affect the importance of caring for your body? Write about that.

2. Re-read "Embodied." What do you see when you look at yourself in the mirror? What have you done to avoid seeing your own physical body? Have you grown more comfortable with your body over the years? Write a poem about your body image.

3. Re-read "learning to breathe." Survivors of sexual abuse often find that during stressful situations they hold their breath, just as they did during the abusive acts. What triggers this response for you? When do you need to remind yourself to breathe? Write about that.

4. Re-read "They Say." As a survivor of sexual abuse, do you tend to see all of life in terms of that abuse? Do you analyze all your actions through the lens of the abuse? Choose one or more of your everyday activities and try to see them totally unconnected with the abuse and write a poem about that.

5. Re-read "Lies I Tell Myself." What are some of the lies you tell yourself relative to your body? Name them.

6. Re-read "Going to the Hairdresser, and Other Acts of Courage." Do you avoid situations that require

being touched, particularly by a stranger? What situations cause you discomfort? Write a poem describing your discomfort with being touched by medical personnel or others who are performing legitimate services that require touch.

7. Re-read "Wonderland." Now that you are years beyond the abuse, have you found that your interest in sexual topics seems adolescent even to you? Have you forgiven yourself for having that interest? Write a poem trying to capture the wonder that an adolescent would have regarding sex.

PART V

RECOVERY, SUBSTANTIAL
HEALING

Everyone's recovery is her unique story, lived not only in the hours at a therapist's office nor in the workings of her own mind, but in her daily living among people who know her agony and those who don't, people who lend support and those who tear at her every success, children who depend on her even at her weakest moments, people who inspire her to grow and those who undermine her hard-earned self-confidence, people who barely know her who sometimes give far more than those she once depended on for life itself, people who love her or hate her or who are completely indifferent to her presence. Recovery takes place in the towns and in the homes where the abuse transpired, or in a place far away chosen because of its dissimilarity to the place of haunting memories, or here and there in no place in particular, wherever a healing atmosphere exists. Recovery can be a long, painful, drawn-out affair that seems never to end, or it can come in a powerful instant that forever changes one's life. Recovery begins at the moment one is willing to say, "I have been damaged by what someone else did to me, and I will no longer give that person complete control over my life as he has had all these years. My life is my own and I am going to begin to live it now."

That moment came for me when I was thirty years old, married, at home with a one-and-a-half-year-old toddler, my oldest son. In spite of my most gallant efforts at being Supermom, I had been aware almost from the moment of his birth that I had absolutely no idea what I was doing. I loved him with all my heart and I was terrified that I would fail him. I was exhausted by my own efforts to do this job perfectly; I was isolated, distrustful, downhearted, and depressed. I wanted more for this child than I had ever dreamed of for myself, and I awoke one day realizing that if I ever expected to provide for his needs at all, I would have to face the realities of my own situation. And so I landed in a heap in my doctor's office, and excruciatingly haltingly told him my story.

Telling him about the physical abuse at the hands of my mother was not so difficult, as I had long before come to understand that her abusiveness was due to her inabilities to cope with the stresses of motherhood and life in general. I had forgiven her for her human failings. Telling him about the sexual abuse by my father was much, much harder because I had not separated myself from that and was still incredibly protecting his good reputation. But I did finally mumble the truth, my head bowed, shoulders hunched forward, two fists clenched between my knees. My doctor gently took both of my hands in his, and although it was I who willingly straightened my spine, it felt as if he had lifted me, and I don't believe I had ever before made such deep eye contact as I did at that instant, and I knew that he cared for me, accepted me, and judged me innocent.

For a little over two years, I counseled with our family doctor on a regular basis. We did not talk about my inner child nor cry for her lost innocence; we picked me up right where I had fallen and worked with the material I had to set me on the right path. We looked at my strengths, not the least of which was my determination to be a better parent than either of mine had been. Slowly I stopped talking about my parents' problems and began concentrating on my own. This was my life and my family I was dealing with now, and I was under no obligation to please my parents, to protect them, nor to explain myself to them. Ironically, however, I did try to please and impress my doctor with my great strides at following his counsel. He, at least, could be pleased, whereas my parents never had been, and his model was of such a high quality. I felt really good about being able to attain the goals he and I had set in regards to my parenting and personal growth, and his values were consistent with what I had believed to be my own.

In the course of counseling, I came to know my doctor's faith, and it was he who clarified for me the mysteries of Christianity, which had always both intrigued and frightened me. The best way I can explain it is that I knew I needed God's saving grace in my life, but I also believed that before I dared to step into his presence I would have to make myself perfect. What I learned is that if any of us were able to do that on our own, then we wouldn't need a savior. Christianity finally made sense to me, and relieved this perfectionist of the need to work so hard at being perfect, because, in the end, Christ had already done that for me.

Assured of that, I became more willing to take some risks. While many people run when afraid, I am paralyzed by fear, and having lived for over thirty years in a state of constant fear, I had essentially not moved an inch. I began finally to stir, my steps as tentative at first as those of my toddler son, and, believe me, I fell as often as he did, scraping my knees, bruising my forearms, and certainly wounding my pride. I was grateful for the people around me who applauded my progress and I felt anger toward the people who mocked me and sneered at my mistakes. At times I clung too tightly to my mentor and wailed betrayal when he pushed me firmly away. I was probably asking of him what my husband should have been providing, but at the time, Jim was barely involved in my recovery, although I had tried very hard to include him by telling him about my sessions with my doctor and by initiating conversations with him about the issue I was struggling with. Jim didn't want to hear about it; I would get through one or two sentences, and then he would change the subject. He surely wanted healing for me and encouraged me to get the help I needed, but he was overwhelmed and frightened by the magnitude of the task, and made it very clear to me that this was my problem.

Jim and I did walk some common ground together. It was after the birth of our second son that I made my Christian commitment and became active in the church Jim had joined four years earlier. Jim and I both grew spiritually in the nurturing and freedom-giving arms of our church family. We were fortunate to belong to a church that is open to a wide range of theological, social, and political opinions, and our family, now grown to five with the birth of our third son, flourished. We studied and discussed faith issues in our home, in our church, and with our friends. I felt vital and whole, as if I had found my place in the world. But spiritual healing is not the same thing as emotional healing, and in time it became evident that I still had long to travel. My relationship with God had been restored and I had found meaning and direction in my life. I had connected to my roots, deeper than my ancestors, and had a sense of belonging to history. I had never experienced that before, and had lived every day as if it were merely another twenty-four hours to survive. Now I had a grasp of the eternal, from the beginning of time to forever, and I felt a part of it, a valuable part.

I am deeply grateful for my spiritual healing, for it has allowed me to move on to psychological healing. The greatest task of recovery is discovery, and I had much to learn about my inner self as well as the world around me. It had been nearly twenty years since I first began my recovery process when I began a round of rather intense psychotherapy, still completely conversation-based. During those twenty years, I flew with the angels and crawled like a worm; I knew soaring success and abject failure; I recognized both support and betrayal; I tried new things, retaining some and rejecting others; I witnessed the unfolding of the lives of my three sons, from infancy to young adulthood; I worked at three different jobs; I established new relationships, maintained positive old ones, and severed destructive ties; I experienced the deaths of both of my parents. I have lived, and for all its ups and downs, living has been far preferable to the sleepwalk existence I had known before that day that marked the beginning of my recovery. At times the recovery process was so profoundly painful that I wondered why I was subjecting myself to it; numbness, at least, did not hurt; but neither was it living, nor was it real. Whenever the pain became too great, I reminded myself that I was doing this for my children, and eventually I was able to admit without feeling guilty about it that I was doing this for myself as well, because I deserve to have a life of my own before I die.

Robyn was hidden beneath many layers of insulation and a stack of masks. As I began to get to know myself, I really liked what I found; I have good strong values; I believe in what John Bradshaw calls a deep democracy, very demanding of individuals to support each other in their commitments to decency and mutual acceptance, granting people the space they need to grow and to become the best they can be. I believe that freedom to be oneself depends ultimately on accepting the responsibility to guard everyone else's freedoms; that if I interfere with anyone else's freedom, I give up some of my own. I believe that power must be granted freely, and never taken by force. I believe that every person on this earth is equally precious to God, and we are all damaged by the corruption of one soul. I believe that responsible adults need to teach children what is right and wrong, lovingly and respectfully by example.

I believe that I have been richly blessed by the presence of many, many good and beautiful people in my life. I have chosen my friends well, but it has not escaped me that providence has surrounded me with a plethora of good people to choose from. In the early days of my recovery, it was easier for me to attach myself to the good people around me and to love them for their good qualities than it was for me to accept the same good qualities in myself. My husband, my friends, my doctor, and a series of ministers became my mirrors, and when I looked at them I saw pieces of myself that I could love. Eventually, I learned to separate and to love them for who they are and myself for what I am, but that did take a long, long time. I am grateful for their collective patience with me and their honesty in letting me know when I was getting too close, too dependent.

During my twenty-year period of recovery, there have been several amusing side trips back into my developmental history to grasp essential pieces of childhood and adolescence. For about ten years I was an avid doll collector: baby dolls, cloth dolls, porcelain fashion dolls, and collectors' dolls. I made dolls and made clothes for purchased dolls out of the laciest and most feminine fabrics I could find. At its height, my collection was well over one hundred dolls, all displayed on shelves in Jim's and my bedroom. Dolls led to teddy bears and other stuffed animals, and our bedroom more resembled a child's room than it did that of an old married couple. I had a dollhouse on a trunk in the corner of the room and a collection of miniature tea sets on my dresser. I now have given away all but three of my very special porcelain dolls, but I absolutely needed to recapture the little girl in me who loved dolls as a child but did not hold onto them. Reclaiming them was instrumental in my reclaiming myself.

At the age of forty I reclaimed my adolescence. That was a particularly rough period in my recovery, as my husband still had not gotten on board. He was still overwhelmed by the problems of my past and did not wish to deal with them. His support manifested itself in the form of encouraging me to go more and more to our doctor for help. The problem was that I needed to rely less on my doctor, not more, so I ended up feeling very much alone, as if I had to carry the entire burden by myself. That was when I quite accidentally heard an old Neil Diamond song on the radio, "I Am . . . I Said," and I connected to music and poetry, two powerful forces already inside me that I had ignored and denied. I spent five or six years having great fun as the quintessential fan, writing letters, making and sending gifts, and attending concerts to which I carried bouquets of flowers for the performer, and sang and danced and screamed just like the teenager I had never been. I became a collector of Neil's music, his photos, and memorabilia. When I bought a CD player, I once squandered three-quarters of the week's grocery money on a dozen CD's that I just had to have. This was pure, unadulterated delight such as I had never had before, and I did connect with Neil Diamond himself, never face-to-face, but I do have several personal notes from him that I treasure. His music gave me something to hold onto that completely changed my relationship with my husband. We began talking to each other, in meaningful ways, and Jim began to understand that I had needed to talk and grow with him, not merely with professionals who are trained to deal with the results of abusive childhoods. We don't always need expert advice or someone to solve our problems for us. Sometimes what we need is to be held and listened to, and to be assured that someone we love, someone who loves us, understands us. Once Jim and I connected verbally, we also began to connect physically, and for the first time in our then eighteen-year marriage, we began to learn how to make love.

The music and poetry not only connected me to Neil and to my husband, but it provided my mind with a link to my heart. For the very first time, I began writing my own serious poetry. That occurred ten years into my recovery period. What a difference that made! At last I had a voice, self-expression. Believe me, it was liberating! But I didn't just plunge into writing about my deepest personal issues. Very few of the poems included in this book were written then, and those are probably recognizable as some of the weaker poems in this book, though I had good reasons for including them. It would be five more years before I began writing the hard poems, five years of sailing along, having a good time, and beginning to act like and believe that I was completely healed and had no work left to do.

Was I ever wrong! At the age of forty-six I ended up going for my first bona fide psychotherapy. I had counseled with my family doctor and several ministers, and I don't in any way diminish their efforts and work with me. They were wonderful, and everything they did with me was just that much less I needed to do in psychotherapy. I read ravenously and had read countless books on the topic of childhood sexual abuse and I took from each what I needed. I had recreated bits and pieces of a childhood and adolescence, but I still needed much help in regards to my emotional state in adulthood. It was no longer possible to deny that psychotherapy was the answer; it was either that or to continue for too many more years unhealed.

I was proud of making it on my own, so I didn't dare ask anyone for recommendations of a therapist. I selected one totally at random from the phone book, long before the days of on-line reviews of professionals. I was lucky. I worked characteristically hard in therapy. Through my first year of sessions I was doing only a little substitute teaching, so I could devote myself to the therapeutic process completely. My family was totally supportive of what I was doing and made many adjustments to accommodate my appointment schedule as well as the financial demands of this commitment.

The same resistance that had kept me from seeking counseling had prevented me from buying into anything that smacked of labeling or a prescribed order of dealing with issues of sexual abuse. While I may have been willing to admit my need to see with new eyes, I was quite unwilling to have anyone tell me what I was supposed to see. On principle, I denied being in denial, but eventually I had to concede that denial stood squarely in my way of further recovery. I have both the capacity to be highly organized and the inclination to be scattered, and what I resist is external imposition of structure. My therapist granted me the freedom to order my own healing process, and what I devised became the outline of this book.

The first step was to recognize and acknowledge the damage incurred in my family of origin. I needed to assess that damage, identify my early coping mechanisms, and determine which of my strategies were no longer effective. I needed to understand what payoffs I was receiving by choosing to remain damaged, and to look for the greater reward that would come from a commitment to total healing. I needed to develop a plan for the repair work that would involve daring to try new things and making emotional and physical connections with people I had kept at a distance. I needed to define proper boundaries and learn how to defend them, balancing desirable vulnerability with necessary self-protection. I needed to know who Robyn is, inside and out, to love her and to trust her judgment.

Six months into psychotherapy I took the most significant step in my healing process: I began writing this book. I had a subbing assignment that day in the computer lab, and the kids knew what they were doing and needed only my presence, not my assistance, so I spent the day on the teacher's computer, devising the outline for this book. The very first poem I wrote is the first poem in the first chapter, "Don't Be Afraid." And I never turned back. I wrote one poem and then another and another. This work has been the most healing, healthy work I have ever done in my life. From the very beginning, I planned to publish this work as a therapy handbook, to be used in the healing process by women who have shared the essence of my experience. I have learned more than I can possibly contain in the lines of this text or the lines of my poems.

As the pages began mounting higher and higher, it actually seemed like the dream just might become reality, and if publication were in the cards, there were some people in my life who had a right to be forewarned. Whether I publish or not, my children needed to be told the truth about me and the grandfather they never knew. Jim and I sat down with each one individually and told the story and what I had been working on in my therapy and in my writing. Each immediately gave me his full support. They were glad to finally know the details that they had only been able to guess at, and Jim and I were pleased with their response. It certainly helped them understand me and forgive some of my more obvious blunders as a mother. When I told my oldest sister about my childhood experiences with my father, she was stunned, but had no reason not to believe me. The dismantling of the invisible wall between us has strengthened our relationship. I have talked more openly about the abuse, and it does get easier every time I say the words. The initial revelation to an individual is still difficult, but no one has ever reacted with anything but compassion, and after that I can talk to that person without choking up. Nearly everyone has encouraged me to continue writing and to pursue publication.

Shortly after I began therapy, I accepted a teaching position in a school that I have loved. Part of the school was built in the early 1920's, part in the late sixties, and part since I arrived there. Walking through the halls is like strolling through a seamless avenue of history, and the atmosphere exudes the best memories of the past and the best promises of the future. This school, so much like the elementary school that had provided my safety as a child, has become home to me and has afforded me the opportunity to give something back that once was given to me. There I have grown intellectually, emotionally, and professionally. Perhaps it was just the right time for me, but more likely it was the people who were just right, creating the correct ratio between what I gave and what I received. Surely it was not perfect, and even that fact has been good for me, for I have learned to accept imperfection and to see the world as incomplete, still in need of work, to which I can dedicate myself. I have known both joy and pain at my school, and have learned from each experience. Mostly, I moved beyond myself into a world filled with children who welcomed what I had to offer them, and who gave me much in return.

Twenty years of struggling through the issues of sexual abuse is a very long time, all of it necessary, but I have finally found that my world is much bigger than that. There is a world beyond myself and my pain, a new world bustling with children trying to grow and find their place, a world filled with people who work hard, each in his or her own way, to make a difference to others. There is adulthood beyond dolls and 8" x 10" black and white glossies. And it asks me to be authentic, to give what I have to give, to ask for what I legitimately need, and to love with a forgiving heart.

I no longer define myself by my abuse. The interesting paradox is that I was much more defined by my abuse when I denied it than I am now that I can talk about it openly, and I was much more controlled by my abuser when I denied his power over me than I am now that I have recognized and named it. I have abandoned my silence strategy for the far more effective behavior of communication. I am still learning to express verbally my fears and anger and disappointments, and at times I revert to tears to let people know that I am hurt, but even that is a vast improvement over swallowing my feelings completely and allowing others to do whatever they wished to me. I am learning to trust my own eyes and to love what I see in the mirror. I am learning to love others for who they are, not narcissistically. My expectations of life now include pain and disappointment, and I am learning to deal with them. I am also learning to expect pleasure and fulfillment. I am learning to desexualize touch so that I can hug and hold without feeling guilt or pain. I am learning to enjoy intimacy with my husband.

I am significantly healed. The healed adult needs to step away from the pain of childhood injuries and walk confidently, upright, looking the world in the eye, living life, and loving it. The healed adult can look in the mirror and see herself and know that she has survived the very worst that life can throw at her. She is strong; she is beautiful; she is real. She knows more about life than she ever learned from fairy tales or Hollywood movies. And she can smile genuinely and embrace the people she loves. She can laugh when she wants to and cry when she needs to. She can give and receive love and forgiveness. She can be a vital part of a trusting relationship. She can look at her scars without terror or embarrassment, and she can handle new wounds, ministering to them with intelligence and understanding. She can express her needs and wants and disappointments appropriately, and she can admit that she will not be "finished" until the day she dies, and she is in no hurry for that to happen. She welcomes new information, new ideas, and new relationships. She is engaged in the learning process and is open to hear what others tell her. The healed adult remembers but forgives the past and welcomes the future with optimism and excitement.

I Don't Know How

I don't know how to talk to people.
I don't understand the subtleties
Of social conversation
That seems to connect people
Much more deeply
Than its superficiality would suggest.

I don't know how to relax
Even with people I ought to be able to trust.
I am always guarded, vigilant,
Observing body language,
Analyzing and interpreting conversation
Through my own paranoia.

I don't know how to let go,
To release the past and move on.
I haven't figured out
That what I'm holding onto
Can never be made right
So I might as well leave it behind.

I don't know how to risk
Trading the comfort of familiar pain
For the possibility of true fulfillment.
I still need to learn
That I am the only person alive
Who has even a whisper of a chance to grasp
    my dreams.

CONTAINED IN MY BRAIN

Contained in my brain
my problems seem
to fill the universe
they somersault
slowly crowded
one over another
the same thoughts
recycled
varied in form

Contained in my brain
there is no light
of fresh approaches
nothing new
nothing creative
just the same old stuff
rehashed reheated
sweaters unraveled
and knitted into mittens

Contained in my brain
there is no life
the air is stale
and replete
of all its oxygen
used up ages ago
while I still had the energy
to inhale and exhale
exchanging breath with the world

Contained in my brain
are words of truth
that must be spoken and heard
exposed to light and air
shared with vigorous minds
who can offer to me
modern solutions
to my ancient
weary problems

Contained in my brain
my secrets engulf me
but if I release them
from my prison
free into the expanse
of the atmosphere
they will be intimidated
by their own smallness
and they will be tamed

CHAOS

My world is chaos now
Cluttered with outgrown toys
That trip me up
As I try to negotiate the path
From long ago to tomorrow

I kick them aside
But they tumble right back
Under my feet, stubborn things
But I must forgive them
For they have nowhere else to go

Shall I sweep them away
And stuff them into
Thirty-gallon green plastic sacks
And toss them onto the heap
Of humanity's landfill of rubbish

Surely this is not all junk
But a casual disarray of waste
With an occasional nugget
An antique of great value
To be prized and guarded

My Friend, will you help me
Appraise all these items
For I am inexperienced
And I cannot distinguish
That of worth from that of no merit

My Friend, will you show me
How to arrange the treasures
So that I may appreciate them
And use them to guide me
And to give me pleasure

IT

1

That nameless thing, omnipotent, ever present,
As dreadful as Yahweh that we stand in mortal fear
Of being caught with "Its" name upon our lips,
As if to utter the word would strike us dead.

"It" is some vague collection of events, mystifying,
Unchronicled and purposely left unclear
To protect the guilty at the expense of the innocent,
To preserve the comfort of an unwilling listener.

The victim doesn't want to talk about "It."
Friends and family really don't want to hear about "It."
Society doesn't have a clue what to do about "It."
And so "It" lives on through yet another generation.

Why do words hold us this way in terror?
Are we yet so controlled by primitive superstition?
Have we granted "It" supreme godly power over us
By submissively refusing to speak "Its" name?

"Sexual abuse," "Rape," "Molestation,"
"Incest," "Fondling," "Sodomy."
They are only words, and words are no more ugly
Than the conspiratorial silence that allows "It" to thrive.

FEELING WITH A LIMP

I walk upright straight
Without crutches or cane
My eyes focus near or far
With just a little help
Of corrective lenses
(I am over forty after all)
My hearing is unimpaired
I am overweight
But otherwise rather healthy
But I feel with a limp

I have stopped cursing God
And blaming my parents
For my affliction
My imperfection
It never did me any good
It only paralyzed me
Indeed it thwarted
All my therapeutic efforts
Delaying and limiting
My recovery steps

So I have accepted my handicap
And gotten on with the business
Of working around it
By befriending people
Who will tell me the truth
And help me to grow
Modeling right feelings
And forgiving my blunders
For I still feel with a limp
But I'm getting better every day

ONLY WORDS

Words cradle me in tender security
As Mother's overburdened arms
Are unavailable to do.
They kiss the tears from my cheeks
And assure me that I am never alone.

They are my friends who uphold me.
They will not abandon me
Nor betray my trust;
They will not deride me
Nor toss me into the fire.

Words are my covenant with tomorrow
Freely granted without reserve,
My promise of a hope
When all reason to hope has been extinguished,
My bridge, my link with eternity.

They are my vehicles of forgiveness
Of unimaginable violations
That have tortured my body
And have sought to entomb my spirit
And to crush my injured soul.

Words are breath for my aching lungs
That never have learned to inhale life,
Inspiration that lifts my eyes
To capture the pure light
Glinting on the mountaintop's snow.

They are a healing balm
That strengthens my resolve
And imparts the indomitable courage
To rise again and again
To create a more hospitable world.

Words are the unbreakable thread
Woven through the fabric
Of all my days,
Stitching them together as a testimony
To the power that only words can hold.

SOMETHING TO SAY

The old man spoke
About his childhood
On the family farm
And he told me about
Droughts and floods and hailstorms
And he was proud
Of how he had survived hardship
With grace and dignity
And I listened to him
And respected him

He told me about the Depression
And how scarce money was
And how hard it was to procure
Even the basic needs
Of food, clothing, shelter
And he was proud
Of how he had survived poverty
With grace and dignity
And I listened to him
And respected him

He told me about the War
And of fighting for what's right
Of watching his friend die
A mere twenty feet away from him
And of the pain of his own wounds
And he was proud
Of how he had survived war
With grace and dignity
And I listened to him
And respected him

I finally gathered the courage
To open my store of memories
And I announced to the old man
"I have something to say"
And I told him how my mother
Had ignored my emotional needs
How she had beaten me
When she could not handle
The demands of parenthood
And how my father had violated me

And I was proud
That I had survived
Neglect, violence, and abuse
With grace and dignity
And the old man told me to be quiet
For to speak of such things
Would bring shame
And dishonor
Upon me and my family

I'M IN HERE

I'm in here.
I've been in here for a long, long time,
Wanting with all my heart to get out,
To be in the open where people can see me,
To tell the world who I am.

I'm in here.
I'm bricked in behind these walls,
Transparent like one-way mirrors
That I can see out of
But no one else can see in.

I'm in here.
Living and growing and changing,
Filling this space completely
So that if I am to grow any more
I must burst through these walls.

I'm in here.
I'm scratching and clawing at the mortar,
Pushing at the bricks with all my strength
Trying to dislodge them,
Trying to tear them down.

I'm in here.
The bricks are loosened now
And there are windows of light,
Expanding all around me,
The walls shrinking lower, lower.

I'm out here.
I'm free to move and free to speak,
And now I can be seen and heard.
I'm surrounded by scattered bricks,
Memories of my incarceration.

THIS IS MY REALITY, AND WELCOME TO IT

I wash the blush from my cheeks
Scrubbing peach foundation
From the surface of my skin
Mascara streaking oily
Brown/black shadowed mauve
My face spotless now au naturel
Stripped of all pretense

My scars are visible at last
To any who would dare to look
And I invite you my brother
To behold the me behind the mask
Damaged, yes, but healing
My skin too delicate now
To bear cosmetic weight

Do not ask me to masquerade
Through yet another decade
For I have already given five
Sacrificed for the sake of my torturer
Himself dead already ten years
And I left aching to live honestly
Free from these thespian rags

You prefer to view him in costume
In full theatrical grease paint
Playing the role of a hero
A brave and gallant cavalier
Noble and patriarchal
His reputation above reproach
An actor reciting lies

And you choose to condemn me
To a similar fate
By closing your ears to my speeches
By denying my wounds and fractures
My bruises and abrasions
That can do you no harm
But can continue to consume me

So turn away if you must
To avoid suffering the spotlighted truth
About him and about me
But do not bid me
To hide among the shadows of my reality
For this is my only moment onstage
And I have already wasted half of it

JOURNALISM

I can tell you:
Who? When? Where? What? and How?
But I can't tell you: Why?
I can only surmise
That in his weakness
He ravaged me
In order to feel powerful,
But I do not know
Enough about him
To determine the roots
Of his lack of strength.

Why did Judas
Betray Jesus with a kiss?
Why did Hitler
Hate the Jews enough to have them killed?
Why did Susan Smith
Drown her two small sons?
Why do men
Pay prostitutes for sex?
Why do women
Leave their husbands and children?
Why can't we all be strong?

It might help me
If I knew
Something of his history
To understand
Why he abused me.
It might make it easier
To forgive
His human frailty;
It might make it clearer
That his actions
Had nothing to do with me.

But I waited too long
To ask my journalistic questions,
For all the witnesses to his life
Are gone now, just like him.
Perhaps some of them knew
Where the flaws in his character
Came from;
Perhaps he hid the truth
From every one of them;
But whatever they could have told me
Is lost to me now forever.

So what does it matter?
I am grateful for my memories.
Too many of my sister survivors
Have only fragments
And those, hazy at best.
My memories of:
Who? When? Where? What? and How?
Have always been very clear.
So what if I don't know why?
At least I know
The origins of my own wounds.

PAPER TRUTH

speak
and your words
float invisible
vibrating the air
the shape
the tone
of your voice
uniquely striking
tympanic membrane
the meaning
of your message
comprehensible
interpretable
misquotable
forgettable
untrue

write
and your words
fuse with paper
bonding
dark to light
visible
images received
upon the retina
transmitted
by optic nerve
decoded
by the brain
ripe with meaning
venerable
memorable
true

Shipwreck

Fledgling ship
Not yet seaworthy
Her fragile frame
Splinters against
Crushing swells

Inestimable treasure
Spills from her hold
Drifting, settling
Coming to rest
Upon the ocean floor

A captive of the sea
No longer free to sail
She becomes
The unwilling dwelling
Of parasites, predators

She waits, she waits
Enshrouded by darkness
Rust crusting over
Her anchor and chains
Turning them frail

Years of salt
Razors of urchins
Abrasions of sand
And force of tide
Tear at her boards

Trash and treasure
Bed together
Mishmash
Waiting to be salvaged
To be reclaimed

No amateur operation
Deep, deep, delicate
Requiring much knowledge
Expert skill
Infinite patience

Each unit to be raised
Carefully, gingerly
To the surface
Exposed to the light
Its value defined

Sparkling gems
Culled from masses of rubble
Silver and gold
Gleaned from mounds
Of worthless matter

Tons of garbage
Separated from ounces
Of jewels and crowns
Her goodness, her soul
Saved from the watery depths

RECONNECTING THE CIRCUITS

Wire snippers:
I'd found them to be
A most useful tool
When I was a child
Subjected to physical
And emotional tortures

Wire snippers
Could instantly sever
Those tiny nerves
That connected
My feeling
To my brain

With the circuits cut
All my experiences
Could be handled
By my intellect alone
With no interference
From my unreliable emotions

I lived disconnected
Not only from the pain
I could no longer feel
But from joy
And pleasure
And love as well

I lived disconnected
From my husband
From my children
From my friends
But still with the memory
Of needing human contact

I lived with the desire
To reconnect the wires
I had snipped
In self-defense
But I had no tools
With which to work

With some expert advice
And my own strong will
I began to repair my circuits
Twisting together
The raw ends
Of long-unused wires

Once connected
Impulses began
To flow once more
Through the wires
From nerve endings
To my brain

At first
It was shocking
And the wires
Burned hot
And I was tempted
To shut them down once more

A power surge
Might completely blow
All my circuits
And I would have to
Begin to reconnect
All over again

I learned to regulate
The amount of current
I allowed
To circulate
Through my system
A little at a time

I persisted
Repairing and repairing
Getting used to
The buzzing sensation
And allowing it to flow
Through my whole body

My circuits are complete
Transporting my feelings
To my brain
Keeping me alive
And healthy and whole
Causing my light to shine

DECIDING TO GROW

Feeble roots
Barely able to do their job
Of absorbing
Life-sustaining moisture
Of transporting
Minerals to the stalk
Weak and withered roots

The stem decides
To be strong and healthy
And to grow
Thick and tall
Reaching for sunlight
Stretching toward heaven
Deciding to grow

Resourceful leaves
Harness their creative power
Photosynthesizing
Their own substance
With truth and light
To conceive beauty
And to persevere

Fragrant blossom
Deceptively delicate
Unfolds deliberate and slow
Revealing herself
To any who would love her
Bearing the treasure
Her seed of new life

Robyn Apffel

DON'T TELL ME HOW TO HEAL!

Don't tell me how to heal!
Don't tell me to get in touch
With my inner child.
Some day I may find her
And hold her in my arms
And give her comfort,
But I'm not ready to do that;
First I need someone to hold me.

Don't tell me how to feel!
Don't tell me to be angry
With my father, my abuser.
I need to feel peace and love
And security before I can handle
The threatening feelings
Of anger and indignation,
Before I can feel fear.

Don't tell me what to do!
Don't take the control of my healing
Out of my hands.
You may know the answers,
But I won't be ready to hear them
Until I figure out the questions,
Until I can trust you
Enough for me to ask.

Let me walk slowly
Until my legs are steady and sure.
Some day I will run
And I will catch up to you;
I will reach my destination
Even if I must travel
In a roundabout way
Along uncharted paths.

I respect your knowledge
But you must understand
That I am not you.
I'm not just being obstinate;
I need to have control
Of my own actions, my own thoughts,
My own feelings, my own life.

So don't tell me how to heal!
You may tell me your story
But please don't presume
That your story remotely resembles mine.
Listen to me and support me
And hold me when I cry.
Most of all, honor my courage
To heal in my own way.

THE STONE

She clenched the stone in her fist
right where her father had placed it
forty years before when at the edge of the desert
he sent her forth alone unprotected
to find her own way to the Promised Land

She had never even looked at it
but she knew by its weight
by its cold coarse density
that the stone she carried with her always
was infectious and dirty and ugly indeed

Four long decades she wandered
with little to sustain her
no Moses to direct her steps
no cloud nor pillar of fire to lead
only her instinct and intellect to guide

The stone slowed her progress
rendering her incapable of the simplest tasks
of shaking a hand or embracing a friend
of playing her music or writing her rhymes
of grasping a cherished dream

But her determined feet
continued the trek across the desert
bringing her at last
to the Jordan's heartening banks
with the Promised Land near in her sight

She waded as far as she could
into the sacred refreshing river
but at last she had to swim
across the deeper waters
to make her way to the other shore

The stone she carried with her
acted as an anchor
weighing her down
preventing her from cupping her hands
to swim effortless and free

The stone was so much a part of her
that she did not know
if she could even survive without it
but to hold onto it now
would surely surely cause her to drown

With the same resolute will
that had delivered her thus far
she uncurled her fingers from around the stone
and for a moment she looked at it
as it lay lifeless impotent on her palm

She let the stone fall from her hand
and as it drifted with the current
to find its place in the muck
at the bottom of the river
she swam safely to the shore

METAMORPHOSIS

She wiggles belly to the ground
Suction-cupped feet gripping the earth,
Yearning with all her heart to fly,
Afraid to surrender her familiar crawl.

She consumes bitter dry leaves
A captive of the treetops
Knowing great height but no freedom,
Teased by a seductive illusion of love.

Threads of her conflicting emotions
Tangle her past with her present,
Encasing her in a chrysalis,
A limbo between being and being more.

Time and faith and miracles
Transform her substance slowly, slowly,
As she becomes the very creature
That God had always intended her to be.

Her shell outgrown and more fragile
Than she had ever supposed it to be,
It cracks, splits open, and she emerges,
Soft, wet, and thankfully vulnerable.

Tentative, she pumps her feeble wings
Forcing life and knowledge through her veins,
Reaping confidence with each success,
Absorbing courage from the sun.

She knows! She knows how to fly!
She allows her wings to take her
Beyond the limits of her imagination
And she drinks the sweet nectar of life.

SHORT CUT

That was my hair
Ash brown strands on cream-tiled floor
Four inches long in clumps
That would be swept away
The moment I was out the door.

It was quite on impulse
I decided to have my hair cut that day
No appointment necessary
So I asked permission of no one
And just walked in and had it cut.

Short and layered and straight
Like I had wanted it last time
But had lost my nerve at the final instant
And had asked for eight inches cut off
Instead of the desired twelve.

I see my face in the mirror now
And my eyes are bigger and brighter,
My smile warmer and more genuine
Than it has ever seemed before
Hidden beneath massive curls.

It pleases me when acquaintances
Compliment my new appearance,
But they don't have the vaguest clue
How thoroughly I had to change inside
To choose to have my hair cut short.

A Lot of Answers

I've been counseling with you for, what?
Three years now? Four?
I've listened to everything you've had to say
And I've depended on you for guidance.
And now you're cutting me loose?
How will I stand on my own?

You've been standing on your own
Right from the beginning.
You walked into this office on your own two feet,
As much a stranger to me
As I was to you,
And you told me your story.
You decided what to tell
And how and when to tell it.
I took all my cues from you
As you ordered our sessions.
You indicated your level of comfort
And we never moved on
Until you were ready to do so.

But what will I do when I'm scared?
I mean, you held my hand
And encouraged me to risk
Speaking, feeling, moving;
You helped me rise above my fears,
Especially my fear of touch.

Yes, and you have done all those things.
Here, you spoke with me
And then you went home
And spoke with your husband,
Your children, your brother,
Your sister, your friends.
You told them your truth
And you asked them to support you,
And when some of them refused,
You stood tall and did not fall apart.

You have given yourself permission to feel;
I didn't do that for you.
You have embraced the full range
Of human emotion, shrinking from none,
And you have shared your empathy
With friends and family
In spoken words and comforting touch,
And likewise you have received from them.

But what am I to do in new situations?
We haven't practiced everything, you know.
I don't know how to act
In lots of different places,
Especially with people I don't know.
What will happen if I make a mistake?
What if I should fail?

Then you'll learn from your mistakes.
You know that you always learn more
From your failures than from your successes.
Think about it: if all you ever do is to get things right,
How will you ever grow from doing that?
So, you make mistakes, and you will learn,
And the next time you will do better.
Nobody expects you to know everything;
We are all human, after all.
Why should you expect yourself
To be perfect every single time?

So relax. You are ready, I know it.
You are going to do just fine,
Not perfect, but just fine.
Learn to forgive yourself, get up, and move on.
You have my phone number.
I'm not going anywhere
And I will not stop caring about you,
But it would be the most uncaring thing for me to do
If I were to hold you back now
When you are so ready to stand on your own two feet.

It sounds like you're saying good-bye
And pushing me out the door.

Yes, that is exactly what I am doing,
And you will thank me for that.

I'M NOT FINISHED

Please, waiter, don't clear my place;
I'm not finished yet.
There are so many things
I have not tried
And others I'd like to reconsider.

I have tasted the bitter
And I have craved the sweet;
The sour has intrigued me; but I have fled, frightened,
From the lusty hot and spicy.

I have settled for bland,
Safe and adventureless,
Afraid to try anything daring.
But I am willing now
To challenge my taste buds.

So bring me a banquet,
A sampling of life,
Grain and dairy,
Fish, poultry, and meats,
Fruits and vegetables and even desserts.

THE MENU

I get to choose?
After all these years
Of swallowing fear
    and guilt
    and shame,
Someone finally tells me
That I have a choice!

I might have chosen anger
Or righteous indignation,
Assertiveness,
    Decisiveness,
        Forcefulness.

I can elect courage
Or strength or power
Instead of meekness,
    Weakness,
    Submissiveness.

I will select
Forgiveness over bitterness,
Affection over heartlessness,
Empathy, not distance.

I should choose
Security,
    Self-confidence,
    Pride;
Effectiveness,
    Fearlessness,
       Resilience.

I have the right to choose
Activity from the menu
Instead of lethargy;
Or a willingness
To be involved in life
Instead of trying to escape it.

I no longer have to ingest
Numbness,
    Emptiness,
      Passivity,
        Paralysis.

The menu includes
Cheerfulness and wonder,
Festivity and fun,
Laughter, playfulness,
And joy.
Where have they been all my life?

I long to embrace
Intelligence and maturity,
Cognizance and discernment,
Logic and perception.
I want to reach for
Acclaim and distinction,
        Excellence,
                Honor,
                        Even fame.

I need to choose
To speak my mind
And release through my mouth
Words of truth,
        Goodness,
                And moral principle,
Instead of stuffing down
Rage and pain.

And if I find
The selections on this menu
Are too limited,
I can choose to walk out the door
And seek another establishment
Where the menu options
Are more to my liking.

A New Pair of Glasses

Damn glasses
They used to work
Focusing inward at least
Introspective
Microscopic observation
Of my own little world

Looking now
Outside myself
All is a blur
Indistinct objects
Hazy, unclear
Rendering me dizzy

A new prescription
Bifocals perhaps
To show me how
To reconcile close up
With far away
Belief with reality

A new pair of glasses
To open to me
A panoramic view
Universal in scope
Unbounded by
Previous perceptions

CALL ME ROBYN

I don't want to wear
My soul on my back pocket,
A designer's label
That proclaims to the world
A stereotype,
A caricature
Of who I might be.

I'm Robyn.
I'm a complex individual
Made up of all my history,
 all my thoughts,
 all my imagination,
 all my feelings,
 all my dreams.
I am living
 and growing
  and learning
  and changing.

So, please,
Don't paste a label on me
And then believe
That you know who I am.

THE PRODIGAL SON
Luke 15: 11 – 32

Father, why do you run so eagerly to greet me?
Why do you reach out to me
To enfold me in your loving embrace?
I have disgraced you.
I have taken all the treasure you so generously gave
    to me:
My life, my talent, my friends,
My knowledge, my money, my health;
I took them all and wasted them.
And your name, Father,
I took that, too,
And used it when it was to my advantage
And denied it when it could be used by other men
    against me.

I have abused and exhausted all your gifts.
Now I have come home to you empty,
Asking for nothing
But the opportunity to serve you,
Yet knowing that even that is to ask
For more dignity than I deserve.

But I see you running toward me
With an intense, forgiving love in your eyes.
I can't believe that this love is for me.
Is it the same love that always was there
Or has your love for me grown while I was away?
Have I finally dared to see it
Or can I see it because I have finally dared
To love you in return?

Father, why are you honoring me so?
You are restoring to me all that I once had;
No, even more than that!
I have been unworthy of the poorest of your treasure
And now you are giving to me the best.
Give the best to my brother; he deserves it.
While I was out seeking my own pleasure,
He remained close and faithful to you.
He will resent me;
He will not understand why you give me such favor.
How can any of us understand, Father?
Our love is so shallow, our forgiveness so incomplete.

Your grace surrounds me.
I fall to my knees before you,
Not daring to look even as high as your feet,
But your grace surrounds me
And your boundless love lifts my eyes
So that I may behold
The radiance of your face.

THE LOST SHEEP
Luke 15: 1 - 7

I tried to follow you, Lord,
But I couldn't keep up.
Your path is so steep and I stumbled
And I was afraid to ask for your help;
I didn't want your help.
There was another path that led me away from the fold.
It was wide and clear and very easy;
The grass was sweet, the flowers fragrant,
The water plentiful, cool, and refreshing.
I continued on and on, downward,
Until the path trailed off to
Nothing
And I couldn't get back up.
All around me were thorns and cracks in the earth.
It was a dangerous place,
Cold, dark, treacherous,
So I crouched behind a rock and kept still and silent.
Then I saw you, my Lord,
Coming down into this awful place.
"You don't belong here; it is too dirty,"
I thought.

Yet you remained, surrounded by all this filth,
And gently called my name.
I am ashamed, Lord.
I have caused you much trouble.
I was weak and careless and untrusting;
Still you cared for me
And came for me
Because I am your own.

NEVER FAR AWAY

Where were you, my Lord,
When my soul ached for someone to hold me,
For someone to understand me,
For someone to take me away from the harsh realities
    of this world?
I needed to be lifted out of my despair,
But instead I was plunged into it deeper, headlong,
Without a prayer of escape.
Why didn't you carry me away, my Lord,
To the peace and perfection of your Kingdom?
Why did you leave me here, alone, afraid,
Incapable of looking reality in the face?
I wanted to see your face, my Lord. Where were you?

I was there my child, right by your side.
I was in the middle of your reality.
You didn't see me because it was not me whom you
    sought.
You wanted a cocoon, but I gave you a cross;
You wanted permission to sin, but I gave you truth
    and righteousness;
You wanted escape, but I gave you life;
You wanted to see only part of my face, but I showed
    you all of it:

Yes, the easy perfection of divinity,
But also the very human face
That knew pain, agony, uncertainty, thirst,
  disappointment.
You have been nowhere that I have not also been.
I was never far away from you, my child,
Only as far as you were holding me from you.

BIORHYTHM

Some people spend their whole lives
Resting on the tops of mountains
And they don't even know
How high up they really are;
All they know is mountaintops.

Some people spend all their lives
Deep in the shadows of the valley
Surrounded by virgin hill slopes
Their feet will never tread;
And all they will ever know is rock bottom.

Some people walk the mediocrity
Of smooth, mid-level plateaus,
Never experiencing high nor low,
Traveling always in straight paths;
The only thing they know is flat.

But me? I climb mountains!
Up one side, down the other,
Then to muddle awhile on the canyon floor
Before my eyes glimpse a new peak
And I must begin to climb again.

I know every elevation
From Death Valley to Mount Everest!
My feet have touched all manner of terrain
In all expressions of weather
In every time and season.

My contentment lies in both
The exhilaration of the summit
And the depth of depression,
And every altitude in between,
The ups and downs of my reality.

I love climbing mountains!
The challenge from the base
Gives me something worth reaching for;
The view from the peaks is breathtaking;
And the climb is life itself.

WHAT I NEED TO LEARN

I teach
Twelve-
Thirteen-
Fourteen-year-olds
And I am learning
So much from them!

I'm learning
To relax
And not take myself
Quite so seriously
To laugh and smile
And to just have fun

I'm learning
To let go
Of the pain
Of my adolescence
As I watch them
Struggle with theirs

I'm learning
To try new things
Without the fear
Of looking foolish
Or of not being able
To do them perfectly

I'm learning
That I don't have to
Know everything!
I can rely
On other people's
Knowledge and abilities.

I'm learning to grant
To each individual
A sense of belonging
In his own place
Under the sun

I teach
Self-esteem
Self-assurance
And self-confidence
I teach
What I need to learn

HOME TO MY HEART

So many years I have lived in my Head
Thousands of miles away from Home
A visitor experiencing Life through reason alone
Slamming the door on feelings and locking it tight

Home is where the Heart is indeed
And I was determined to stay far away
For the Heart is a painful place to live
Filled with memories of Trust betrayed

The Mind at the very least provides comfort
In its sterility uncompromised by Love
In its certainty uncomplicated by Hope
In its objectivity untouched by Pain

But although my Head is teeming
With facts and figures and even fantasies
It is at its very core quite empty
Completely devoid of the Meaning of Life

Meaning is not to be found in encyclopedias
Nor in the relationships of math or physics
But in the affiliation of humanity
In the gift of Trust and the granting of Forgiveness

I have been so afraid to risk again the Pain of Betrayal
Afraid to hope for the security of true Love
Afraid to leave the emotionless soil of my Head
To go Home to the Vulnerability of my Heart

And yet I have ached for Love a tender touch
I have yearned to give deep and enduring Friendship
I have been weary of this intellectual hollowness
Where everything makes sense but no one feels

FACES

Faces . . . thousands, millions of them.
I never saw them before
As I walked through life
Solidly planted behind my own face,
Looking always inward,
Avoiding the eye-to-eye contact that demands
Attention, recognition, commitment to love.
I was afraid to know those faces
So different from my own,
Afraid that if I saw them
I would become them
And lose a part of myself
To those strangers outside of me.

But one day I was compelled to look at one face,
Just one.
I studied that face minutely and found
That it was beautiful.
There were years of living engraved on that face;
Struggles, tears, hurts, fears,
Joys, love, triumphs, hopes;
All had made their mark,
All were there for me to read.
The story told in that face was not my story:
It belonged uniquely to someone else.
I could behold that face, I could touch it,
I could even change it by becoming myself
A piece of its history;
But I could not become that face nor could it
    become me.

Knowing that one face did not diminish me in the
    least;
Rather, it intensified me;
It freed me;
It invited me into love,
A love that can only be found outside of myself;
It challenged me to look into other faces,
To touch other souls,
To seek, to accept, to give and to receive love.
That single, beautiful face opened to me
A sea of faces,
Thousands, millions of them,
Each belonging uniquely to someone else.

SPIRITUAL CONNECTION

I have never looked into your eyes,
Neither have I touched your hand;
I have never spoken my thoughts to you,
Nor have my ears heard your voice speaking to me;
I have never been near to you
And you wouldn't know me
If you saw me in an almost empty room.

Still, I know you
And feel with you a spiritual connection,
For I have heard you sing
Your own words that express
The very essence of your being.
Those words have spoken to my soul
And have made me alive
To the thoughts and feelings
That I share with you,
Convictions that we hold in common,
Dreams that carry us along the same road.

You have fulfilled a purpose in my life
To bring me closer
To my God
And to the people I love,
To help me dare to say
What I think and feel and believe,
To give me the courage to share myself with the world.

Somewhere, I know, our souls have touched;
Perhaps some day
You will be as aware of that fact
As I am.

DREAMLESS SLEEP

Waken me, Lord, from this dreamless sleep.
It is too dark, too long.
I'm sliding down through time
Too fast
With nothing to hold onto.

I've seen your light;
It warmed me into life.
I've heard your sweet music;
It soothed me into trust.
You gave me dreams long before I ever knew you,
Before I knew that you cared for me,
Before I let myself care for you.
And now they're gone.
The light is gone;
The silence suffocates me;
Dreams elude me.
Please, Lord, restore me into your presence.

I hear music, Lord! Sweetly, softly at first;
Now vibrant! I'm listening.
There's a voice!
It's not your voice, Lord,
But it is the voice of one who loves you.

The words lift me
Into the light of your being;
They carry me close again to your love;
They speak the same dreams
That first led me to you.

Lord, you did not abandon me to a life
Without dreams.
Your dreams abound in this world
In the music, in the words, in the voices,
In the love
Of those who choose to follow you.
I hear them, Lord.
I am awake.

IF I SHARE MY TEARS

Smiles I share so easily
With friends or loved ones
Or people I don't even know.
Trustless smiles protect me like armor
Deflecting words that can wound,
Deeds that can damage,
Emotions that can kill.
Smiles stand between you and me and touch.

Tears I save for solitude;
They're mine, and I hold to them dearly.
I fear they will wash away my privacy
And expose me to your love.
Vulnerable then, shall I allow my tears
To fall into your heart?
Will you treasure them
And add to them your own?

If I share my tears with you
It must be only that I trust you
To treat them tenderly
And to understand
The pain from which they flow.
If I share my tears with you,
You will know that I have entrusted with you
The most delicate portion of my soul.

Waiting for Me

I stood alone waiting for love,
Not knowing where to look,
Not daring to reach out my hand,
Not hearing love's whispered invitation.
I waited silently, speaking to no one,
Denying that I needed
To touch and be touched,
Disclaiming the compassion
That my heart knew it held.
I waited in darkness,
For my eyes refused to see
That love has always been
All around me.
I waited
And I wanted,
And all the while,
Love was waiting for me.

Love was waiting for me
To open my eyes
And see its presence
In every moment, in every soul,
In every situation.
Love was waiting for me
To hear its sweet music
Calling me to respond
With my own song.
Love was waiting for me
To hold it in my arms,
To gently caress it,
To give it comfort and assurance.
Love was waiting for me
To stand by its side
So it would not have to wait
Alone.

I LOVE WHAT I AM

When I look at you, I see myself
And for the first time in my life,
I love what I see.
I've spent a lifetime trying to hide,
Covering, pretending,
Playing a thousand different roles
So no one would see me as I really am.

When I listen to you, I hear my thoughts
Echoing what my heart knows to be true,
And I love what I hear.
I have always walked through life
Appearing so confident,
And yet afraid that if I spoke my mind,
Someone would know me as I really am.

When I feel your touch, it feels like my own,
As if you were a part of me,
And I love what I feel.
In the past I had always run away,
Protecting, avoiding,
Erecting impenetrable walls of steel
So no one could get close enough to hurt me.

But you have shattered my defenses;
You have breached my security;
You have tried all my keys;
And you have opened all my doors.

And now I know myself as I never have before
And for the first time in my life,
I love what I am.
It was always there, just
beneath my thin façade,
Waiting, hoping,
Struggling to survive just long enough
For your love to make me free.

As If It Should Matter

I write my life as if it should matter
To anyone else that I have breathed
The oxygen that surrounds this planet,
The very element that supports the being
Of president, prisoner, reptile, flame.

Why should anyone care to know
How I have hungered and thirsted
When he also has ached from emptiness
And endured the fire of a tongue
That begged not for surplus, but survival?

What can anyone learn from my words
That could possibly assist him
As he travels the paths of his own life
So different from mine that one would wonder
If our steps are indeed taken on the same earth?

Can I be so arrogant as to believe
That others may be profoundly touched
By my expressions of agony and triumph,
When for so long I have shut my ears
To the voices of my fellow-travelers?

I write my life not to instruct
Nor to draw a map for others to follow;
I write to illustrate common feelings
Hiding beneath the surface of details that make each
    life unique.

I write my life as if it should matter
That we are all connected to one another
By the silver threads of emotion,
Threads that cannot be broken
By time nor distance nor personal experience.

JIGSAW

It has taken me all of my life
Just to get this much of the puzzle together,
Only to find that some vital pieces are missing.
I started logically at the corners
And worked across the top, down the sides,
Then along the bottom and in toward the center,
Placing as many of the pieces as I could,
Identifying a pattern, matching colors,
Joining designs, filling spaces,
Trying to make everything fit.

The picture lies flat on the table,
Two-dimensional, not at all like life,
With faces broken in jigsaw lines,
Separating features that belong together.
Gaping, empty spaces, patches of nothingness
Stare back at me, accusing me
Of carelessness, laziness, and neglect;
Demanding that I try harder
To find the missing pieces, wherever they are,
And put them in their proper place in my life.

Yet I know that I have looked everywhere,
In every pocket, in every recess of my mind;
I have exhausted every possibility
That lies within my heart and soul.
Where else can I look? What else can I do?
In desperation I pull the pieces apart
And reassemble them in different ways,
Each new attempt producing interesting results,
But each one still unfinished, incomplete,
With huge holes begging my attention.

I must look elsewhere for those pieces,
Somewhere beyond myself, beyond my own knowledge.
I must look in the hearts and minds
Of other people, who have seen and heard,
Who have thought and dreamed and done
Things that are far beyond my own experience.
I must accept the love that others offer me
And incorporate their golden pieces
Into my own puzzle of life, adding that third dimension,
Joining my pieces together with theirs.

I'M NOT THAT EASY TO LOVE

Just as you promised, you have given your love only to me
And I know that I'm not that easy to love.
I don't mean to,
But I know that I test your love daily,
Even moment-to-moment,
As my mood catches you unaware of how to act with me,
What to say, what not to say;
As my activities steal away the moments
That you had hoped we'd spend together;
As the love, time, and energy I have committed to others
Leave me with precious little to give to you;
As my insecurities ask more and more of you,
Half-expecting you to say, "No,"
But always sure that you will continue to affirm me.

I find myself wondering how far I can wander
Before you withhold your love,
Just like a child trying to define limits;
But I know your limits,
And though I may flirt with the danger
Of crossing outside the bounds of your love,
I do not step over the line that will divide me from you.

I need your stability,
For my own leaning is toward roller coaster rides
That cause my emotions to plummet then soar,
That take my mind into castles in the air or into their
    dungeons,
That leave my body tingling with excitement or exhausted
    from fatigue,
That fill my soul with intimate communion or drain it to
    isolated loneliness.

I need your perseverance,
For I discourage easily and give up
When the task is too difficult for me to perform alone.
I need your sense of reality,
For my own perceptions carry with them
A good portion of my hopes and dreams
And do not always conform to what truly exists.
I need your human touch
To erase the loneliness from the depths of my soul,
To warm the coolness of my surface emotions,
To caress the fears and cares and tension from my body.

I need you to tell me of your deepest thoughts and feelings
So that I may know you fully;
I need you to listen to my deepest thoughts and feelings
So that you may fully know me.
I need the security of your promise,
For it frightens me to think of life without you
And I know that I'm not that easy to love.

GROWING TOGETHER

You seem to understand that one person
Cannot give me everything I need,
And I thank you for that.
You give me all your love;
You give me security and fidelity;
You give me comfort and support;
You give me the space I need
To move and to grow,
Giving to and receiving from others.

The trust you and I have shared
In our twenty-five-year marriage
Has allowed both of us great freedom
To form relationships
That add much to our lives,
Both separately and jointly
With no jealousies coming between us
To undermine the relationship
We have built with each other.

It is your very nature
To be totally, unconditionally accepting
Of everything I do or am.
I need others to challenge me
To become better, stronger, freer,
And to move in fresh directions
To experiment with life
Finding mountains to climb
And new worlds to explore.

I share my findings with you, excitedly,
For I relish change and newness,
And you accept my gifts
With both hands open,
Realizing that together we are stepping
Beyond the bounds of our mutual past
Irrevocably into the uncertain future
Where you and I will surely become
More married than ever before.

You Were with Me

You know me well after all these years
Of sharing our lives in marriage.
You were with me through the awkward uncertainties
Of the newness of intimacy;
Through the doldrums
Of intimacy grown familiar and then cast aside;
Through the exhilaration of intimacy reclaimed.

You were with me through the brash uncertainty of
   my youth,
When the fragile outer shell of complete confidence
Tenuously concealed my inner core of insecurity.
You were with me when my success shored me up
And when failure eroded my foundations.

You were with me when I needed your support
And you stepped aside when I needed to stand on
   my own.
You were with me at our children's births
And stayed with me as we muddled along with them
To establish a family built on love, respect, and
   mutual commitment.

You were with me when I doubted
The very existence of God
And when I was struck like a bolt of lightning
With the absolute conviction
Of his being, his love, and his abiding presence.

You were with me when times were hard,
When winter storms raged outside, when inner
    turmoil tore at our souls.
You were with me when times were easy,
When balmy spring warmth smoothed over rough
    seas,
When sunlight and rainbows filled our hearts.

And I know for certain
That at the end of my days here on earth
I will be able to look back over all the days of my life
Since the day we married
And say that you were with me.

AFTER EIGHTEEN YEARS
OF MARRIAGE

I didn't know what would happen
When I decided to start enjoying sex;
I didn't even know how to do that;
I only knew that after eighteen years of marriage,
Something had to change, and it had to be me.

It had been too easy for both of us
To comprehend why sex was so unpleasant for me,
But that understanding only served
To perpetuate the dysfunction
Of the sexual part of our marital union.

Our mutual commitment to the marriage,
To our children, to fidelity,
To patience, persistence, and responsibility
Had held us together in spite of
Our disappointment in unfulfilled hopes of intimacy.

It was time now to decide:
Would we walk forward hand-in-hand
Or would we move ahead in different directions?
I didn't know because I didn't ask you
How you would react if I changed.

One night I just risked letting go
Of my inhibitions, of our ancient script,
And I made up my mind
That I was going to enjoy your touch
And participate in our lovemaking.

And you certainly did notice the difference
And you responded in kind,
Warm and pleasant and loving,
Still gentle, but passionate, connecting.
Finally, after eighteen years, we were married.

UNVEILED

Not even tulle, but veiled in linen
Head to toe covered
Hidden from view, protected from touch
Estranged from her own devoted husband
By her unwillingness to risk exposure

And he accepting of this separation
Believing it can do no harm
To live on parallel planes
On congenial forward paths
That move through time uncrossed

She breathes mummified air
And resists pressing against
The restrictiveness of her bandage wrappings
But her mind comprehends
That this is not what marriage ought to be

So she unwinds miles of crisscrossed strips
A tangle of unfulfilled hopes
And unrequested pain
Revealing a tender body in need
Of the balm of fresh air and love

She stands unveiled before her husband
Wounded but with a strong will to survive
And in his eyes she is
The same beautiful young woman
He saw her to be many years before

Indeed, he has always seen her so
Warm and lovely and loving
Strong enough to help him face
The ugly truths of her life
From which they both need to heal

CLOAK OF INNOCENCE

With both hands gently
I push the wide-banded hood
Back away from my face
Tugging the drawstring bowknot
Unbinding the tie at my throat
The cloak draping loosely
Over my shoulders
Into deep folds at my feet

I pull a loop over its button
Unfastening the front
Of my white woolen cloak
One hundred percent virgin lamb's fleece
Once pure and soft warm comfort
Now yellowed by the years
Stained by tears and reality
Tattered and worn thin

I hold my cloak wide open
For you to see its scarlet satin lining
Never before revealed
With not a pretense of innocence
But an urgent invitation
For you to take my body
As I release my cloak
And it falls honestly to the floor

THOU SHALT

Thou shalt crave thy husband's touch
For it is right and seemly to do
Thou shalt delight in his kisses
And take comfort in the warmth of his body
Close to thine
Thou shalt taste the salt of his skin
And savor its uniqueness
Knowing only him but knowing him well
Thou shalt explore every inch of his body
Until thou touchest every feature
Every fold every pore
A billion times over
Yet thou shalt always want to discover him more
Thou shalt allow him to come into thee
And thou shalt welcome him
And treasure his presence
Thou shalt hunger to be one with him
And thou shalt love him
With all thy heart
With all thy soul
With all thy mind

CLOSER TO LOVE

Alone in self-containment, with a tongue that could speak
But with a will that refused to communicate,
She sat with words cramming her mind,
Private memories clogging her heart,
Precious dreams longing to be fulfilled.

Speech beckoned her and teased her tongue;
He invited her to stand and walk and move away from
    herself.
He praised her feeblest efforts
And he applauded her halting progress;
He listened to her fears and failings.
He did not judge her as he spoke to her in words of
    encouragement
And gave her the assurance
That Trust, though sometimes risky and always self-exposing,
Is closer to Love than living locked within oneself.

Alone in darkness, with eyes that could see
But with a soul that refused to perceive,
She stood with hands tight as shutters against her lovely
    face,
Holding inside her valuable identity,
Denying admittance to all foreign elements,
Unable to distinguish between enemy and friend.

The Light sought her and pursued her;
He forced her to focus only on him;
He wrapped himself around her and would not let her go.
He searched her and found her weakness
And he penetrated that pin-point hole in her armor.
The Light grew steadily within her until he encompassed
    all of her soul
And gave her the assurance
That Truth, though sometimes hard and often painful,
Is closer to Love than living in blindness.

Alone in silence, with ears that could hear
But with a mind that refused to listen,
She ran from everything inside her
That was too painful for her to bear.
She ran fast and far with no particular destination,
Only the determination to escape her memories.

The Music overtook her and he surrounded her;
He held her in his arms and he comforted her.
He understood her pain and he accepted her aspirations.
He released her from her past, gave her a home in her
    present,
And encouraged her to hope for a future.
He provided the sustenance that would help her grow
And gave her the assurance
That Freedom, though often overwhelming and demanding
    of great devotion,
Is closer to Love than living enslaved by deafness.

Alone in isolation, with hands that could feel
But with a heart that refused to be vulnerable,
She lay in ambivalence,
Blanketed with layer upon layer of insulation,
Holding it tightly around her,
But aching to be free of it.

Touch stood patiently by her side and would not violate her.
He waited for her to emerge willingly from her cocoon
And then he caressed her and kissed her
And became one with her.
He was gentle and responsive to her needs.
He spoke to her truthfully, sang to her sweetly,
Listened to her intently, shared himself with her
     unreservedly,
And gave her the assurance
That Intimacy, though sometimes frightening and always
     courageous,
Is closer to Love than living alone.

TIME AND PLACE

Of all the moments since the beginning of time,
Of all the places in all the world,
God chose this time and this place
For us to share.
By God's own hand,
Our paths crossed
At the very instant you and I were there to meet.
We saw in each other's eyes the spark
That he intended for us to save
Only for each other.
Our minds met there on the path to our future
And took hold of one another's
Hopes, dreams, fears, cares.
You took my hand and walked with me
Not on your path nor on mine,
But on a brand new road,
Unknown to us both,
Prepared by God for us to walk
Together.
Our souls touched and were bound by love
In this time and in this place
That God chose for us to share.

REFLECTIONS ON GIFTS

Baby's first toothless grin . . .

The day that Baby holds his spoonful of mush up to
Mother's mouth . . .

Little handprints cast in plaster to weigh down papers
on Daddy's desk . . .

A sack full of marbles . . .

A fistful of violets . . .

Red and yellow and orange leaves pressed between
two pieces of waxed paper . . .

A bottle opener bought with his own money . . .

A puppy . . .

A radio . . .

His first watch . . .

Washing dishes . . .

Cleaning the garage . . .

Mowing the lawn without being coaxed, nagged,
bribed, or paid . . .

That first kiss . . .

An engagement ring . . .

Oneself given in marriage . . .

A home . . .

A baby, the gift of love that two people give to each
other . . .

A lifetime of dreams shared, promises made and kept,
anger swallowed,

Smiles, laughter, tender caresses, confidences,
    heartaches soothed,
Transgressions forgiven, compromises, sacrifices . . .
A whisper in the final moment of life saying,
"I have always loved you more than I was ever able to
    tell you."

THE PEARL

She never wanted to be
one pearl on a string of many
but yearned instead
to be a member
of something more universal
a crown of gold
bejeweled with diamonds
emeralds and rubies
studded with sapphires
and she the pearl
not at the center
brilliantly sparkling
yet visibly present
softly glowing
an integral part
of the beauty of the crown

My Own Hero

I had never trusted myself
So I looked to you to be my hero,
Someone who would rescue me
From dangers real or imagined
And carry me to safety and freedom.

In you I found the courage I needed
To face uncertainty and shadows.
Your bravery quelled my fears
So I could walk steadily by your side,
Gaining confidence with every step.

How your imagination intrigued me!
The more I listened to your dreams,
The more vivid and creative my own became,
Stretching far beyond my timid barriers
To transform fantasies into realities.

Your vitality grabbed me by the heart
And sent me whirling, dancing into life,
Daring to try new things, to explore,
To reach beyond my grasp,
To learn all that there is to know.

I admired your intellectual approach
To the complexities of daily living:
Philosophy, psychology, theology
So congruent with my own opinions
That I began to believe that I could be right!

You touched me with your sensitivity
To my deep, private pain
And I responded by embracing yours,
Savoring the saltiness of your tears
Left on my lips by a kiss.

Your gentleness enfolded me
Like a baby's blanket, a mother's arms,
Lending warmth and softness
To my tired soul,
Coaxing me to relax and rest trustful.

I basked awhile in your kindness,
Sweet courtesy extended to me,
And I was determined that all of humanity
Should experience the grace
Of living in harmony and peace.

With unbounded generosity you shared with me
All the truths you have learned,
Challenging me to abandon
Comfortable but ineffective ways
In order to grow and become the best I could be.

I have seen you work faithfully
To assure that what you believe,
What you say, and what you do
Are all one and the same,
And I value your integrity as I do my own.

You have trusted me inside your boundaries,
Your vulnerabilities exposed
As mine have been to you.
We have treated each other tenderly,
Respecting, honoring our separateness.

We have loved one another
In pure, beautiful friendship,
Unconditionally, in non-controlling ways,
Granting to one another
The space to grow, the courage to risk.

From you, my precious hero,
I have finally learned to trust myself
Enough to be my own hero,
To believe that I really do have
Something valuable to contribute to this world.

I still do need you, though;
Not to rescue me nor to carry me,
Not to care for me as you would a child
Nor to do things for me
That I can do for myself.

I need you to be my friend,
My soul-mate, my confidant,
Someone who will always tell me the truth,
Who will listen as I struggle to grow
And will share with me joys and sorrows.

THE GROWN-UP WITHIN

Never mind the child within
She's strong
She can take care of herself
She's the one who survived
years and years of abuse
and carried the whole world
on her seemingly fragile shoulders
You needn't worry about her

It's the grown-up who needs
to be coaxed out of hiding
and nurtured and encouraged
to take charge of your life
She's the one who knows
what is good and right and logical
the one who can solve problems
with intelligence and maturity

Don't allow that child within
to hijack you to a land
that is governed by raw emotion
for though she may seem
to have Herculean strength
she does not possess the knowledge
to meet the complex demands
of the grown-up world

So persist in sending messages
until they get past the child
and reach the adult at the controls
who can accurately interpret the signals
and use her cognitive brain
to figure out real solutions
She is the one who has the power
to determine the best course

FIFTY THINGS I DO WELL

Cooking, sewing, interior decorating,
Drawing, painting, calligraphy,
All kinds of arts and crafts,
Photography, embroidery,
Flower arranging,
Cake decorating,
Doll-making, cookie baking,
Dinner parties and kids' parties,
Organizing games and sports,
Word games, board games,
Crossword puzzles and jigsaws,
Travel plans, vacation plans,
Driving a car,
Spending money!
Writing letters,
Writing poetry,
Writing essays,
Children's sermons,
Teaching Spanish, teaching English,
Teaching kids,
Chairing meetings,
Contributing to meetings,
Coming up with great ideas
And carrying through on them,
Observing details,
Finding solutions,
Seeing situations from many perspectives,

Mediating conflicts,
Drawing interesting metaphors,
Communicating clearly,
Encouraging the despondent,
Mothering, wifing, friending,
Giving, feeling, caring,
Loving.
These are fifty things I do well.

WISDOM

wisdom hurts
erupting
through tender gums
swollen with resistance
it squeezes
uninvited
into unenlightened caverns
crowded
enameled illusions
that implore you
to pluck it out
but wisdom insists
on standing its ground
declaring its missive
until the others
tired
decayed and cracked
and worn with time
concede
its superiority
and one-by-one depart
leaving only wisdom
to remain
firmly rooted

THE LIVING WATER

You have changed me, Lord, and I thank you.
I was once a rock, hard and unmovable;
You showered me liberally with your Living Water,
But it cascaded right over me,
Leaving my barely moistened surface
To quickly dry in the burning sun.
Once I was like the desert sand,
Very thirsty for your Living Water,
But I let it slip right through me,
Shifting the glassy particles from here to there,
But leaving their substance unchanged.
There was a time when I was like the thick, stubborn clay
Whose dry, cracked surface allowed your Living Water
    to seep in
Only to be trapped in stagnant pools.
Or I took your pure Living Water
And mixed it so thoroughly with my own poor dust
That all that remained was a muddy stain.

But you have changed my substance, Lord.
You have crushed my resistance
Without pulverizing me.
You have enriched my soul with your own
Life-giving, life-sustaining minerals
And you have sowed in me
Your own strong, healthy seeds.
You have rained upon me gently with your Living Water,
And it is that water alone which is able to release
The goodness you have placed within me.
With your constant care and the loving warmth of your
    sunshine
You have caused life to grow
In the fine, rich soil you created in me.
And, Lord, I thank you.

I'D RATHER BE STRONG

Quite by default I think
I've chosen to remain childlike
For decades beyond what should have been.
Shyness became a habit, an excuse,
For shrinking from social contact,
For shirking social responsibility.

At weddings I'd sit, unmoving,
And never venture beyond my assigned seat.
Even congratulating the bride and groom
In the reception line was painful for me,
And getting up to dance was out of the question;
I was far too self-conscious to join in the fun.

And funerals? Forget it!
There was always some pretext I could claim:
Illness, sick kids, job responsibilities,
Or I could always be out of town.
Besides, I had no clue what to say or do
If I ever did actually attend.

Social gatherings? I don't like crowds.
I don't drink alcohol
And I don't like being around people who do.
I'm really bad at social chitchat;
My conversations tend to be deep,
Which other people find exhausting.

I am fully aware that it is weakness
That prevents me from participating
In normal, everyday social situations,
And I would much rather be strong.
I no longer need to be protected from life;
All I need is experience, and there is only one way to
   get it.

My observation days are behind me now,
So I will kiss the bride and groom and wish them
   happiness.
I will greet family and acquaintances
And I will call them by name.
I will introduce myself to strangers
And talk with them to put them at ease.

I will attend funerals and pay my respects
As I offer my condolences to the bereaved
And share with them pleasant memories
Of their dearly departed.
I will remember that this event
Is surely not at all about me.

I will participate in social conversation,
Avoiding hot topics and choosing instead
To speak of interesting things.
I will ask more questions than I answer
And I will listen more than I speak
So that I actually get to know someone new.

I could go on being self-conscious,
Feeling awkward and embarrassed
To be seen and to be heard,
But I'd rather be strong, mature,
And relate to others around me
As an equal, as a loving and caring adult.

INTENTIONAL LIVING

I'm not a feather floating on the breeze
Falling down, down, spiraling,
Catching an updraft then
Lifting towards the treetops,
Crosswinds pushing me gently, firmly,
Then suddenly dropping me
And watching me fall.

Nor am I driftwood tossing on the sea
Bobbing up and down endlessly,
Fettered to free-flowing waters.
The tides will not carry me
From this shore to another far away,
And I refuse to utter
Words of fear, doubt, or despair.

I am my own engine
And I go wherever I please.
Life is not just something that happens to me
Waiting for me to react,
Rather a work of my own creation,
Planned, revised, perfected, lived
According to my contract with myself.

NEGOTIATION

Marriage most certainly is not a 50/50 proposition
And anyone who claims it is, is simply wrong.
Today, I might get 85% and you just 15.
Tomorrow, you'll get 90%, and I will be satisfied with
    my 10.
On days when we both seek exactly the same thing,
We both walk away smiling,
Each with 100% of what we want.

Marriage is a continual give and take,
Negotiating not for dominance nor control,
But for moments of happiness,
Sometimes getting the better end of the deal,
But never at a cost too dear.

The grand bargain always, always
Places the marriage first and foremost,
And any negotiation for time or for pleasure
Honors the do no harm clause of the agreement
Above all else that might be gained.

TOMORROW'S MEMORIES

Tomorrow's memories need not be
The same as we own today.
We have the capacity for change,
And at this very moment
You and I share the desire for the same.
All we need now is the mutual commitment
To harness our very best effort,
Our very best knowledge and resolve,
And make the changes that we know will lead
To intimacy, honesty, and fulfillment.
Together we can create for tomorrow
The kind of memories we only wish
That we had today. Let's do this.

TOMORROW MORNING

I want to wake tomorrow morning
With you lying at my side,
Both of us breathing the satisfied contentment
Of lovers who have slept peacefully,
Secure in each other's arms,
Trusting in each other's love.

I want to wake tomorrow morning
To the promise of your companionship,
To your presence in our verbal communication,
To sharing our decision-making
And planning for a future
That will span all the years of our lives together.

I want to wake tomorrow morning
Accepting all the challenges of a new day,
Deciding with you not only how to fill our hours,
But discussing what is most important
To each of us separately
And to both of us as a married couple.

I want to wake tomorrow morning
Alert and receptive to every possibility
That lies before us, new and exciting
Opportunities for us to work together
To achieve common goals
And to support each other's individuality.

I want to wake tomorrow morning
With you lying at my side,
Both of us breathing the satisfied contentment
Of lovers who have slept peacefully,
Secure in each other's arms,
Trusting in each other's love.

PREDICTABLE SURPRISES

Nothing in life is as predictable as the unpredictable.
It is never a surprise when rain falls on a parade
Or when ants by the thousands invade an afternoon picnic.
Of course the florist will deliver pink flowers to your
    wedding
When you adamantly requested purple,
And Uncle Harry will surely arrive already drunk.
You will reach the peak of your labor with your first child
At the height of the season's worst snowstorm
When none of the roads between home and the hospital
    has been plowed,
And the vacation of your dreams at the beach
Will be disrupted by the hurricane of your nightmares.
Oh, you can do your darned level best to plan your life,
Putting all the pieces in place;
Completing the necessary educational requirements with
    high honors;
Investing a portion of every paycheck
To secure your family's financial future;
Purchasing insurance for your car, your house, your
    health, your life;
Deciding where to work, where to live, even where to be
    buried when you die.
But life is full of surprises,
So go right ahead and make your very best plans,
But be prepared for the predictable surprises
That surely will come your way.

LIVING BY IMAGINATION

No, no, I'm not talking about living
in an imaginary world;
that would be insanity.
I'm talking about living by imagination.
No, it's not the same thing;
the difference is all in the little preposition.

When life is unsatisfactory,
that is when I live by imagination,
and I begin by imagining
how I would really prefer my life to be,
and, Honey, what you and I are living right now
is very far from satisfactory.

What I imagine for us
is more than love and commitment,
more than companionship and respect,
more than a good working relationship;
I imagine intimacy, communication,
communion, and oneness.

I imagine that you share my vision
of a marriage that yearns for touch
and is not satisfied with less than our best.
I imagine that we are comfortable
enough with each other
to always be forthright and honest
even when the truth may be unpleasant.

I imagine that we will be kind and caring
because there is simply no other way to be
when we speak to each other,
even when we are righteously angry
or hurt or disappointed or frustrated;
I imagine that even then we can be respectful.

When we live by imagination,
we can change what is unsatisfactory
into a new and acceptable reality,
one that gives us both the best
that you and I together are capable of achieving
by making what we imagine into our new reality.

STAGES OF LIFE

All alone
Little and helpless, totally dependent
Moving and growing, still awkward and shaky
Constant motion, ceaseless questions, silly mistakes
Increasing autonomy, even rebelliousness
Finding another and another and another
And then the one to share life forever
Building a nest
Creating little and helpless dependents
Guiding and teaching them the wonders of life
Finding the balance between giving space and lending
    support
Finally letting go and sending them forth
Adjusting to being just two again
Rediscovering joy in one another
Facing pain and illness together
Taking care of one another
Old and helpless, totally dependent
Accepting the inevitability of death
All alone

DURABLE DREAMS

Durable dreams span a lifetime,
Undamaged by time or place,
Undaunted by circumstance.
Durable dreams are enriched by years
Of rubbing the rough edges by hand,
Of gilding the highlights,
Of embellishing the already ornate details.
Durable dreams survive
Affliction, poverty, and failure.
But reality?
Now, there is something very fragile
That needs to be handled with care.

Personal Mission Statement

As I walk through the days of this life . . .

May I be aware
Of the preciousness of every moment.
May I use my time
To learn and to grow in wisdom,
To listen with an open mind,
To feel with an open heart.

May I be aware
Of my physical needs.
May I care for my body
By choosing nutrition over taste,
By exercising regularly,
By resting appropriately.

May I be aware
Of the dignity of my work.
May I honor my commitments
To prepare young people to face the future,
To model success,
To be honest in effort.

May I be aware
Of the infinite value of every person.
May I treasure my relationships
By being supportive, trustworthy, and fair,
By giving with no thought of return,
By guiding, but refusing to control.

May I be aware
Of the uniqueness of my gifts.
May I dedicate my talents
To affirm the goodness of humanity,
To inspire tired souls,
To bring peace into a hurting world.

May I be aware
Of my interdependence with others.
May I have the courage
To share pain,
To bear burdens,
To accept humility.

Writing Prompts for Part V: Recovery, Substantial Healing

1. Re-read "I Don't Know How." What are some of the things that you don't know how to do, things that are holding you back, keeping you from moving ahead in your recovery? Name them and consider alternative behaviors that might produce better results for you. Write about that.

2. Re-read "Contained in My Brain." How do your unexpressed thoughts hold you in the past? How would talking openly about your abuse and your abuser free you to live a more satisfying life? Writing about your hidden thoughts and committing them to paper will breathe new life into your resolve to move ahead.

3. Re-read "It." What power do words hold over you? How comfortable are you using correct terminology when talking about sex or even about bodily functions? What are some of the words you avoid using? Write a poem that uses them.

4. Re-read "Something to Say." Do the people in your life grant you the same freedom to tell your story as they presume for themselves? Is there someone who routinely shushes you when you speak your truths? Claim your truth by writing about it.

5. Re-read "This Is My Reality, and Welcome to It." Have you been living your life as if it's a drama played onstage? If so, who has provided you with the script? How can you change your script so that it reflects the truth? Write a poem about that.

6. Re-read "Shipwreck." Believe that your vessel is filled with great treasure that has been lost in the shipwreck you call your life. Who is in charge of your salvaging operation? A therapist? A pastor? A friend? How is the salvage operation going? Write about that.

7. Re-read "Deciding to Grow." Emotional growth begins with a decision. What resources do you possess that will make growth possible? How can you harness those resources? Explore your options in a poem.

8. Re-read "The Stone." What weighs you down and prevents you from moving easily through life? How long have you been needlessly carrying it? How can you get rid of it? Write about what weighs you down.

9. Re-read "Metamorphosis." What stage of life are you in? Are you still the larva, or caterpillar? Are you inside the chrysalis, changing from larva to butterfly? Or have you emerged from the cocoon, ready to fly? Write about life stages.

10. Re-read "The Menu." When did you realize that you could choose a different way to live? What would you choose differently? Discuss the available choices and make your selections.

11. Re-read "Call Me Robyn." What does your name mean to you? Have you defined it, or has someone else defined it for you? What is the difference between a label and a name? Describe how others have labeled you, and claim your right to be known as a whole person.

12. Re-read "Never Far Away." Have you felt abandoned by God? By your family? By your friends? Honestly evaluate whether your own

attitudes have contributed to your feelings of being alone.

13. Re-read "Home to My Heart." Are you ruled by your body, your mind, your spirit, or your heart? Do you allow all four components to share responsibility for your well-being, or do you close one or more off? Examine how you give control of your life to any or all of these four components.

14. Re-read "Spiritual Connection." Is there someone in your life with whom you have connected on a deeply spiritual level? Write about that.

15. Re-read "If I Share My Tears." Whom do you allow to see you shed tears? Why is it more difficult for you to share your pain with others than it is to share other aspects of your life? When someone close to you dies, are you able to receive comfort from the hugs and touch of others? Write about sharing tears.

16. Re-read "I Love What I Am." Do you love others more than you love yourself? Do you see yourself in others and find it easier to accept their wonderful qualities than you find it to accept your own? Who are your mirrors? Write about them.

17. Re-read "Jigsaw." As you have gone about piecing together your life, have you found that some pieces are missing? Where have you looked for them? Can the puzzle called your life be complete without them? Write about constructing a puzzle of your own life.

18. Re-read "You Were with Me." Who is it who has always faithfully been at your side, through thick and thin? Your spouse? A parent? Some other relative? A friend? God? A pastor? A therapist? Honor that person with a poem.

19. Re-read "Cloak of Innocence." How have you hidden your body from your significant other? Are you comfortable enough now to stand naked before this person? Write about that.

20. Re-read "Thou Shalt." Are there any religious commandments learned early in your life that have erected a wall between you and your mate? Have you ever given yourself permission to engage in healthy sex with a mutually consenting adult? Write about it.

21. Re-read "Closer to Love." Notice how Speech, Light, Music, and Touch change the life of the writer, bringing her closer to Love, but not all the way there. Is there someone or several people in your life who could be represented by Speech, Light, Music, and Touch? Write about that.

22. Re-read "Fifty Things I Do Well" and write your own list.

23. Re-read "Personal Mission Statement." Write your own personal mission statement and make a commitment to yourself to live it.

EPILOG

Recovery from the trauma of being sexually abused, particularly by someone I should have been able to trust completely, has been a lifelong occupation, but it is no longer a preoccupation of mine. Thoughts about the abuse no longer consume my waking moments and they no longer dominate the night. I am substantially, though not completely healed. My metamorphosis began long before I was even aware of it. Like the caterpillar, I had spun my cocoon of self-protection of the material that I had inside me, by instinct, not by intent. Inside that cocoon I was transformed by my innate desire for freedom, freedom from fear, freedom from abuse, freedom to be the very person I chose to be. Now having the freedom to fly, I will continue to experience the dangers that are ever-present in everyone's life, but I am now free to respond with intent and maturity.

Areas in need of remediation will certainly be revealed to me as I continue through life, experiencing new challenges, and then I will deal with them with the same determination with which I have thus far addressed the issues I have already resolved. Everyone's life is an adventure into the unknown, and mine will be no different. Substantial healing merely means that I have learned healthy coping strategies instead of relying on the ones that may have worked during childhood, but which consistently let me down in adulthood; substantial healing means that I am living as an adult, fulfilling my responsibilities to my husband, my children, my family, my friends, and my community. Certainly I still have much growing to do and much left to learn; I will until the day I die, for that is the nature of life itself.

When I took my first tentative steps on the road to recovery, I probably expected to reach my destination in a year or two, but the goalpost kept changing, moving ever further and further from my grasp. At times, the temptation to give up and give in was very strong and I was so weary from the hard work that seemed to offer little reward. I resented others who were exempt from the efforts I had to expend. I railed against the unfairness of life and wondered why mine had to be so hard when others seemed to lead a charmed and happy existence. I was tired of it all, and began to believe that the tiny steps forward I was making were surely not worth all the effort. But whenever I took a well-deserved rest, I always started up again, and walked another mile, and another, and another, starting, stopping, resting, reinvigorating, building up muscles, facing greater challenges, meeting with success after success. Yes, there were many disappointments along the way, many failures, and, no, I have not reached all my goals.

If my story is not yet finished, then why am I considering this book to be? Quite simply, because I know that my story will continue to unfold for years to come, and I have no idea what the next half of my life will bring. Middle age seems the perfect place to end this major chapter of my own life and offer whatever wisdom I have gained from my experience, the abuse, and the therapy to overcome the effects of that abuse. The poems in this book were written over the course of psychotherapy sessions which came to an end when my therapist and I mutually decided that I had completed the work I was there to do. Then I stopped writing, but I did not stop growing or learning, and I do not intend to stop either growing or learning for many years to come.

I encourage anyone who needs to find her voice to try her hand at writing the bits and pieces of her own story.

Words on paper have great power, and it is power that is most needed to combat the effects of being abused. Once a powerless child against an adult abuser, now a grown woman can reclaim the power that was taken from her and use it to enhance her life and make her whole. What never should have happened in the first place can finally be laid to rest so that it will never again interfere with the life, love, and happiness that everyone deserves. Anyone who has survived childhood sexual abuse has already shown great strength in the very act of survival. Having done that, the rest looks at least possible at first, and when taken step-by-step with a qualified counselor, the possibility of healing becomes a reality. Each word of truth spoken by a survivor brings her closer to her goal.

I wish each reader much success in her endeavors to put the horrors of her past into the proper perspective. The sexual abuse that was suffered as a child helped give each one of you the very strength you need to overcome the damage it inflicted upon you. Embrace that strength and recognize it for the gift that it is. And write your own story.

ACKNOWLEDGMENTS

Acknowledgments have always seemed to me to be one of the most important parts of a book, which, unfortunately, often goes unread. Now that I am allowed the opportunity to write my own, I am finding the task both easy and difficult. It's rather easy to decide whom to thank and for what, but quite difficult to appropriately tone down my gratitude to fit within reasonable parameters for a published work. I have concluded that I must privately extend my thanks to each person listed here and thank him or her with the effusive expression of gratitude that is deserved. I will do that.

The lion's share of my thanks goes to my husband Jim Apffel and our three sons, Kirk, Erik, and Aren. Jim has been with me from the time I was an eighteen-year-old college freshman. We fell in love and married and made a life together. Jim always encouraged me to get whatever help I have needed and unwaveringly supported me in my writing endeavors. While some parts of this book deal with survival issues, the large majority of it deals with moving beyond survival towards intimacy with my husband. All I have ever wanted in life was to have a healthy, loving, and intimate relationship with Jim, and that was what I was working for in my therapy and in my writing. I thank Jim for helping me find that.

When they were in their mid- to late-teens, Jim and I told Kirk, Erik, and Aren what my counseling was about and what I was writing. Without a moment of hesitation, all three of my sons gave me their total support, and for that I am both proud and deeply grateful. It was, after all, my love for them that initiated my counseling in the first place because I knew that in order to be the mother they needed me to be, I would have to be healthy and whole. I am absolutely certain that had it not been for them, this book would never have become a reality. I thank Kirk, Erik, and Aren for their love, support, and forgiveness, and for being my pride and joy. They have grown now into fine young men, loving, caring, and compassionate. Each is unique and special, very different from each other, and yet they are very close to one another. Jim and I enjoy their company and they seem to enjoy ours, and for that we are truly thankful. Some day I will have to write the missing chapter of this book, the chapter on motherhood, and give it just to them.

I looked up to my oldest sister Judy Swiencki as I was growing up, and continue to look up to her today. Her footsteps in life preceded mine, and although her shoe size is smaller than my own, I often found her shoes hard to fill. As she has done for her own six children, she has consistently encouraged me to grow and to be myself. My brother Ed Shand was my friend and protector all during my childhood. He let me tag along and made life fun. To this day, he continues to care for the four sisters who made him feel lost in the middle as we were growing up.

Cindy McKee and Kate Weller, Jim's sisters, have given me unconditional love and acceptance, which I have greatly appreciated. When Jim and I met, they were ten years old, but our age difference was completely erased many, many years ago. They knew my history and never treated me as if I were damaged. They truly are my sisters.

My childhood friends supported me in ways that were crucial to my survival, and they never even knew it. I owe a huge debt to Jean Ohlweiler Pirina, Joan Ohlweiler Sisk, Christina Huemer, Elida Nelson Griskonis, Karen MacKenzie, Ken MacKenzie, and JoEllen Shotwell Preylowski.

For many years school was my safe haven, the place where I knew I was cared for and accepted. My teachers recognized my value as a human being and helped me see it. Without their encouragement, I would not have survived childhood intact. They nurtured my greatest strengths and cultivated my creativity. I thank especially my fourth grade teacher Frederick Stradtman, who gave me the self-confidence to think I could write poetry; my fifth grade teacher the late Alan Farner, who attended my wedding and continued to keep in touch with me until his death; my math teacher Richard Johnston, who, along with his wife, welcomed me into his home during summer vacations when I most needed a safe place; and my English teacher Katherine Farley, who gave me a very strong foundation in language and defined the term "grammar school." Two of my high school teachers stand out for their contributions to my well being. Raymond Lalley, my driver's education teacher, introduced me to counseling as a means toward personal growth. David Rein, my English teacher, has been and continues to be a mentor and a friend. From him I learned the finer points of grammar, but I also learned to dare to express myself in writing. Without knowing how desperately I needed it, he offered me refuge in his home, where I always felt safe, and treated me with dignity and respect. I still value his friendship and enjoy visiting him annually.

Karen King, Jeanie Maksymovich, Maggie Reluzco, Elaine Gorman, and Laurie Ruch have been good, supportive friends who have given me much in my adult years. I treasure the friendship of Nancy Stevenson, Elaine Smith, Pam Murn, Pelli Wheaton, and Ross Danis, who stood right by me throughout the writing process for this book. They have read every word I've written and offered valuable criticism.

I never would have taken even the first step toward emotional healing without the counsel and caring of my family doctor, C. Lawrence King, a dear, dear friend. He gave me the great gifts of love and faith, and he has been an excellent role model for me in every way. He gave me my voice by encouraging me to verbalize my feelings. His counsel led me through a period of rapid and significant personal and spiritual growth, precursors to all that followed. The first step is always the hardest, taken with fear and trepidation, but Larry gave me all the encouragement I needed to take it, and for that I shall be eternally grateful.

I am indebted to several of my pastors, who guided me personally, emotionally, and spiritually along my journey: Bud Hart, Peter Sulyok, Sue Reisinger, and Kirk Bingaman.

Doug Taylor, my psychotherapist for the three-year period during which the entirety of this book was written, deserves the greatest portion of my acknowledgments. Not only did he move me from fear to confidence, but he is the one who took my poems and turned them into a comprehensive plan for recovery from the abuse I had suffered as a child. He recognized the therapeutic value of my writing and applied every piece, one at a time, to help me find my path toward healing. From each poem, he extracted nuggets of truth and used my own words to guide me through the maze of recovery. I appreciate his humor, his commitment to his patients, his positive attitude, and his sensitivity. Doug handed me the reins and allowed me to direct my own therapy because he recognized my need to be in control of my own life. Under his counsel, I finally grew up.

To all others who touched my life in ways I may not even recognize, I am thankful. Sometimes even strangers or those we meet casually perform little acts of kindness that somehow change our lives. They, too, are angels who cheer us when we're feeling down, lift us when we are ready to give up, and teach us what we need to know. We are, indeed, all in this boat together.